v v v

Doll In The Cupboard

v v v

Yvette Louise Melech

v v v

Copyright 2023 Yvette Louise Melech

This book is a work of fiction. Names, characters, places, and incidents either are products of the author's imagination or are used fictitiously. Any resemblance to actual events or locals or persons, living or dead, is entirely coincidental.

All rights reserved, including the right of reproduction in whole or in part in any form.

About the Author

"Doll in the Cupboard" came to life during an adventure Yvette Louise Melech had when she was suddenly stuck on a Caribbean Island due to an unfortunate weather event. Initially, Yvette was on her way to New York City to meet with other creative friends. Suddenly a hurricane required Yvette Louise to reshuffle her itinerary fast. Her travel agent advised her to head to a Caribbean Island to wait for the hurricane to subside. The love of her life resided on the island of Grand Cayman. Upon shuffling her plans Yvette's love affair tumbled as her lover became ill and was hospitalised. Yvette Louise herself had to undergo a series of ear operations on island as when swimming she discovered an ear tumour.

Post-operation she was unable to fly, and her youngest son was stranded with her. Obtaining the London school headmistress' permission to continue her son's educational requirements on island Yvette Louise turned her life into a positive adventure. Making the most out of the unexpected. Her art company also came crashing down in London since she could not visit. Yvette Louise put her son in a diving class to get his Padi Diving qualification while she endured the skilful surgeon's knife and was wrapped up in ear bandages.

Yvette's lover pulled through his illness with newfound strength. A new ship of life was ready to set sail - creativity during catastrophe brings forth beautiful new beginnings when we challenge ourselves. May love continue to shine – love is always under a palm tree, as is the beautiful gift of poetry some of us are blessed to receive from God's grace. Yvette, as "Doll in the Cupboard," is in the early seeds of creating a new platform in the art world using her poetic gift.

Acknowledgements

My parents for every childhood memory we shared in artistic freedom: Anne Louisa Melech & Bogdan Melech, may you rest in eternal peace.

My children - for every bend we take, we land in rainbows: Cyrus E Melech, George Melech, Richard V Melkonian, Adrian Hart, Veronica Melkonian.

My Aunts: Marianne Pearce Reynolds, Eileen Kemp.

My rediscovered Ukrainian Melech family with our British rock, "farmer Graham."

My American best friend, Victoria Osborn, and my Jamaican best friends, Lavern Scott Esther, Anderson Beverly and Ernie Smart.

Hugh Cecil Hart, for standing by me, with heartbeat's release, for birth of my poetry in 2019

My animals: Bingo Hildare, Spartan, Horace, Aston, and my horses: Picasso, Asti- Charade, who lie in rest

I'd like to express my thanks to all my friends, followers around the world with my utmost gratitude to Kevin Watt from allpoetry for helping me ensemble my first collection of poetry.

God bless everyone who's supported me on my poetic journey.

Contents

A Raven's Announcement 1
People Poison 3
A Man with Two Heads 5
Two Divided Sisters 7
A City Coffee Gathering 9
An Old Swinger Up Town 12
Sitting By the Window 15
Cafe Gossip 16
My Ukrainian Aunt 18
Tempestuous Tastes 20
The Cobbler 21
African Adventures 23
The Bin Men of Belgravia 24
Cleopatra Visited 26
Dead Men's Corpses 28
The Man with the Bloody Hands 31
Spiritual Intoxication 34
A Red Bicycle Stand 36
Dolls News 39
The Crazy High Five 41
Modern Day Paraphernalia 43
Invisible Servant 45
Ducks Quacking Quack Quack 47
Climate Sums Three Men French Kissing 51
In The Evening Light 53
A Man in Green Velvet 54
Three Thousand More Miles 56
Everything Washed Out 58
Tips To Conservatives Heading For PM 60
Bells In the Night Air 61
A Midnight Chase 63

A Parade of Dolls Enemies	65
Personally French	67
A Ritzy Affair With My Dwarf	69
Doggie Bag Tails	71
The Wife's Secrets	72
A Grey-Haired Ghost	73
In The Midnight Air	75
The Dumping Ground Of Bird C	77
An Evil Practice	78
Princess Ukraine	80
The Grey-Haired Ghost (2)	81
The Hand with A Green Fly	82
A Lonely Piano	84
Grandmas Ghost Returned	85
Heartbreak Island	86
Contaminated Contamination	88
Three Men in A Bed	90
The Hotel Porter with a Sly Eye Halloween collection	91
The Spitting Dragon	93
We're All in The Same Can of Worms	94
The Man with The Pipe	95
Artificial Beggars	97
Send Me the Key to My Cell Now	98
The Hamburger Man (adult humour)	100
Chicago Boots	102
Three Cross Dressers	104
Strangulation In the Dark Side	105
An Evening Deck	107
Country Bumpkins (Track One)	108
A Sporting Life	110
Second Stanza the Fly	113
Under The Prickly Thistle	114
In Heavens Name Number Ten	116
Good Old British Farmers	117
Moreish Cream Eggs	119

Only In My Dressing Gown 120
The witches in Greenwich 122
Pulling Strings 123
The Shallow People 125
The Creepy Dudes Wife 127
Green Fingers... 129
The Sky Is Blue 130
In Scotlands Raindrops 131
Lost A Rule Book 132
Coffee Gossip (2) 133
Underneath The Elephant 135
The Haunted House 136
The Man with Dark Spectacles 138
Raindrops In the Night 140
Let The Music Be Your Light 141
Count My Garter.. 143
Porridge on The Sofa 145
Congratulations Pure Jewel 146
A Good Samaritans Wand 147
Blood Moon Chronicles Coming Soon 148
The Farmers Dark Side 149
Lines By the Thames.. 150
Unions Up in Arms 151
Grass Up!... 152
Porcupines And Needles 153
That Is the Question 155
Dracula Lost His Fangs.. 158
The Grinding Road 160
God Save Queen E 161
Blue Murder 163
Coffee Gossip 165
Thou Wicked Lawyer 167
In The Midnight Hour... 169
Daft News 171
The Overcoat...172

Space Flash Station 175
Febzer The Wild Dog 177
Blind Men Who See 178
Come Inside My Dolls Cupboard 180
The Red lipstick 182
Hampstead Heath 184
Yvette 185
Broken Glass 186
A Human Experiment 189

A Raven's Announcement

In the twinkling night sky
London city shuddered by falling stars
shedding memoirs of blonde-haired men
who led by hardened knuckles.
As the world tips upside down.

As night air breathed magical whispering howls
from a dark raven
cloaked in a black-haired spiky number

He sighs as he perched on Tower Bridges watching fluctuating clouds
off Europe's catastrophic pickled onion stew
comprised of French frog's jumping
Behind Germans wagging their tails
Red salami the men in breeches stuffed in gobs
As its hair raising enough to lose one's wig
Todays news as Russians go into caves
Recalculated their new slaves
Whose head is it next?
The dark raven preached

Escargot dripped with heavily soaked garlic
There's not many British
Who are telephone operators now
Robots take calls
The big dark cloaked raven laughed out loud

Under his pointed beak

He speaks

" Ah, a woman's head is on the chopping block now at number ten?"

"Holy Cow, I must spread the word to my fellow birds 🐦 ".

People Poison

I was racking my brain
How on earth do we end up
With poisonous spiders
They're rolling blackjack again
Last night at pomegranates beach
They've got dark black shades on lopsided
Their mouths are dry at one side
Due to a big fat Cuban cigar hanging
Like the scar hiding under a Versace shirt sleeve
Rolled up at the cuff, as they left their gold cuff links
Behind closed doors in a security safe
That's full up with dirty money
All handed down from a skinny dark haired banker
A man everyone meets on the roulette wheel.

This is an in between bat hopping recovery spot.
Watching eyes they've got popping red ones
Underneath the black sunglasses
They're probably by Karl larger-field
If they don't sneer at French snails.

Too of a game makes them partially insane
Cops and robbers look weak
Beneath these blind hypocrites
There the ones at top of the deck

We can lift our own much earthlier bound
Be it brown boots the chemist forty quid shades
Up over our sleeked back and sides
Today my hairs not like the wild witch of the east side.

Tutting our painted red lips
If you managed to find the tube
In your hundred penny bag
That's ten pounds at the pound shop
I haven't even got to pick up a morning newspaper yet!

A Man with Two Heads

Darkness hung down in midst of currents from the Thames rising like dragon's breathing.
T'was by nightfall, when Saturday nights drunks were hung over falling backwards out their beds.
London drug dealers hung about to try hitch a human
On the morning after dark trip.
Weekends cat and mouse games.
In cities overlapping screams.
Down by the river Thames
Where this city splits itself in two
By its seams.
The north south divide of dwellers
Whereupon the Thames is the fort
For all the evil delayed from Saturday night
Where the pumping pimp trying to catch fresh female flesh, for his hungry men in bed
Their pumping balls about to burst unless a vagina is trapped
For thirsty crack cocaine brings many blue pills out old mothers cupboard
The beasts crawl along London's streets
Everything ends up spilling beans on Thames beach.

I cut my herringbone net full of tripe
Jumped up on an old sailor's boat with all my might.
Off we sailed down to Westminster
My hub where I bit off my own dead mothers umbilical chord.
Westminster I ran with my black dog in my hand.

My captain awaited on deck.
Had to escape bloody lunatic attacks
Safe in hand a tall bleached skinny aristocratic man
Knocked on my cabin at seven am
Holding raspberries.
Forgive me in his throat pocket.

Two Divided Sisters

There were two sisters
From two different wives

They don't have any bonding
Whose fault is that?
Ask the big wise white Persian cat
As he sits meowing, he's quite fat
He sits on my blue carpet in the hallway
He's the mousetrap.

Upon a discussion with Horus
my Persian cat.
Tonight by some begotten hour at that!
one's fingers weaved magic until moonlight sings a song
called...
Sweet pea dreams

It comes to pass T's not a farce
Alan Ackeborne's a playwright
Was good at that old lark
So two ugly sisters who were very twisted
both turned out miserable old hags
Through no fault of their own,
I say sitting counting my pennies
in the blue room.

I Give my dog a bone before I re- hunt the cat
He's shifted.
We'll all share at whisperings of haggis with a dash of blue simmering herbs

Imagine the scandal!
Makes Megan Marple look dandy leg dull on the Hollywood billboard ridgeway

The plot to spot herby goes in a twist
'Twas not the wicked stepmother
of the long lanky legged streaked blonde daughter from cote-de-zure rich French quarters
That old mother hen was too busy
Pinning a house onto a French husband she ditched in a rush
Was not of Oxford English school quartets.
Not a student, the granny of madam Twigs legs
worked around a bending alleyway under a bridge

Now she's bunked back in gay Paris
in a chateaux besides a beach
Knock back a piece of haggis as I preach
it's the insides of peeping cattle the sheep are asleep

A City Coffee Gathering

Ion yesterday's sky staying sanely bright
As, no rain clouds opened.
I tiptoed fast around the block
Collected my friend
"Lady Maisie Payton Bailey ".
Dragged her out of bed throwing on an English tweed coat, over her British pale skin.
I then threw her penthouse keys in mid-air.
We locked up her fort well and truly bomb proof
Left her peach greyhound in the set
As we were about to embark on a dog free meet.
Just down the street, around the bend
Where the green, red, white and blue coffee bar lights flash each day.
I had a few pounds found in my old piggybank
However surprise, surprise, rather a few more of the most peculiar glitzy set poured out their dens, as we arrived.
As though? we'd awoken up the town on our determination
To grab a dog free coffee, so we could chat nonsense
Aston, the hound dog, he's a cheeky munchkin at times
Found a way to sneak round my now white garden gate
He's rather fond of Lady Maisie Payton Bailey.
So he joined our gang.

Out of the blue smiling city air, without sign of crying raindrops today.
As, I ordered out aromatic blended caffeine fix

Of various combinations,
for nowadays coffee lists, are like eating a la carte
Such an art form each type
One needs one's eyes tested at times to take in the assorted variations.

However, Lady Bailey is quite a simple type to choose for.
As for me, I'm into all that organic milky oat stuff,
as such.
Soya is one of mine tender points
As we sat under city umbrellas, they were, the cafeteria's own decorations.
Various peculiar folk arose from other bedchambers
Close to this particular set
I've dragged you inside right now
So these were people
Who jumped out of their beds on seeing my lady and I arrive.
A tall bohemian gentleman
Rather closed shop towards me
Very adept at conversation with my Lady Bailey
I believe from my experienced eyes,
that he's from the other side.
One doesn't quite know these days how to define some people, so I'll only but try.
" Long with lanky limbs, dark brown long beard.
Accompanying long wavy hair with an upright moustache.
Wore the attire of a bohemian clam
Yet, quite adverse to females, with an underlying eye for male geezers hopping by.

Yet, he's not one you'd meet at the local barbers.
Looked like a well-groomed other side male specimen.

Then out came Joe a local grunting lord who resigned from the house.
He got tired of meeting other fellows at gentleman's clubs.
Uptown, not down, but I'm in a meantime ground spot.
So, he retired to hop in between property's city investments.
Must have had a dyslexic tuning around his birth time
As his mother groomed his school uniform.
For, he's got one slanted eye,
rather tilting to one side.
A plump rounded face, without any bone structure.
Rather like a blown up balloon.
Looks like he'll go pop anytime soon.
Yet, start a conversation about politics,
or world affairs.
He knows more than the blinking president of USA

So there we all sat drinking coffee
Having a good old chin wag
Ladies'n Lords are my superficial terms

An Old Swinger Up Town

In the old days
Nineteen-eighties
To be precise
We used to disco dance around.
About town.
Checking out,
checking in.
All the boogie spots best slots at our disposal.
Panty liners zipped inside.
Our overnight dance hall bags
Usually comprising of
leather to ride.

Zipped up to the brim.
Our black top hats.
Balanced precisely.
To utmost precision.

Up on top of our over lacquered hair.
Still hanging on in thin lit camera filtering zooms.
Spotlights on par.
Waiting for cues.

Our ringlets hung
Overnight excursions sung through
Good or bad hair days.

Still in recovery from hot hair tongs
like hot riverside's weeping with songs.

Our red pouting lips are now whispering tips.
On how to mix
The sauciest cocktails with evening news.
On the side.
Wearing pineapple pieces in cocktail sticks.
Advocating peace.

Around, around we go
About town, whose table are you on now?

Wearing heels. We sneak inside,
using private members cards.
We scurry like white innocent mice
Me and my three-girl band half did a high kick
strutting our new glossy brand.
Around town
Doing a drag.

Stepping out of a white limousine.
Two of my three chick feathered crew
Didn't half but grin our cheeks off.
I'm telling you!

To nearly half split seams.
Those tight skirts took more than
a good pair of legs to squeeze.

Welcome to our bandstand.
More on par.
After lifting a lid of another jar of
bananas in a jammy jar

Sitting By the Window

I'm a porcelain doll sitting by a window
I haven't cracked up yet
Which is quite surprising
They tried to crack me up those demons
I overrode the wicked.

Now, I'm riding a white horse over mouth-watering human
Guinea-pigs!
They scuffled their overhanging paws sighing dots on lines.
They actually only know when signing a line is imperative
As their choking by an old banker
He's got his charms hanging down
Over an open neck shirt.
It's warm where that lot hang out.
They're all drinking rum as Seine flu sniffs
Be last on the mind of men carrying stale warts
The skin of these dopey dodgers
Be smeared with holes from past infested diseases.

Holes with open pores on these demons faces
They were too busy snorting cocaine
on one sunny day playing with blondes
on Miami Beach.

I'm sitting by my window
With lots more pins but unfortunately no needles.

Cafe Gossip

The coffee scented aromas rose
From a bar down the corner
Of my own back yard.
Morning yells from screaming wives
They'd chucked their husbands
Out the back door.
Maintaining their pride.
As the thunder went bang
Lighting struck at seven am
All the people were dripping wet
Soaking under red umbrellas
Sinking into London gossip wonders
No stirred up the dead yet!
But a local cleaner with blonde bleached hair
Was already sweeping up cigarette ends.

The husband homeless now
He was dancing cheek to cheek
With his tart he'd picked up fresh
Not compressed yet by other men entering her
Be it an underwires bra
Boobs perched up
The cock crowed from pigeons on the hunt
Crumbs from buns lay on floor
An old bag lady has more cash stuffed
Right down underneath her drawers.
Pantyhose wringing wet

Let's gossip on the bench
Whose getting laid on London's parade?
Don't hatch your eggs too fast
You're in for an uncertain blast!
City life is wicked.

My Ukrainian Aunt

My aunt Olga
She's divine
She has a brain like a maestro on wheels
No one is there age in real terms
We're all as young as Fred Astaire
With our rusty dancing shoes.
I had a pair for flamenco once

I'm going to gather up my flock of
Springy sheep
They're not starving yet
But extra hay I must find
For England's green hills weep
Through lack of raindrops
I sit on a London beach and weep for
Loving our world
Yes I do I sob as I pray
Like little Bo-Peep without her sheep
I will fetch, carry and borrow hay
On account if I may
For northern hills nearby my new shack
In dusty dark woods I sat last week
Holds more green grasses for sheep to munch
I once had carted hay for miles
In an old wagon I spruced up like a glitzy tart
Went all over UK in my wagon
Pulled horses on top

To posh spots
Where I galloped over a fine few white horse vale's
Down by Wiltshire
Got my hands cut holding bloody stains
From horses wounds
Just a scratch in a haystack

Back to this joint
Dear sweet Olga Queen of my father's art palace
To England you must come my lady
Your time Is to dine with my country people
Sip sweet red wine
With hamburgers on line
We even got an extra tent in the shed
Pure goat hair produce
It was hitched from a belly dancing bandstand
Over Morocco shores
There's No spring in any venomous snake
That will stop me
Pulling you out of death from serpents
Over the iron wall
The curtains ready to close
But mine is open
Then we'll dance Ukrainian jigs to celebrate!
Hurry up Grandma
Get your wheels oiled
You're coming like it or lump it!
My country people have Ukrainian flags

Tempestuous Tastes

Apart from the finer sides of romantic dining
There's been one or two occasions
I recall throwing one glass of wine over one swine I'd been dating.
Standing up tall leaving a dining hall
That was back in nineteen ninety-four.
The particular geezer eats oyster mushrooms, even now
He's dancing with all the kings' men over at that castle at Windsor.

The next hairy lump of masculine meat I sat opposite
Was downtown in Belgravia
He got strangled across the table
I left my white balaclava on the desk
In rage.
Stood up like a bull
Tipped the table over
Then I spat in his face
He deserved every inch of my rage
Go on turn the next page.
You will need your paracetamol pack on tap
Before I declare my other romantic dining charades
Everything comes out on the table

The Cobbler

I went to the cobbler in town.
Not this town.
A cobbler in another big dusty city,

In going through bags overflowing with my stuff.
I found some favourites immersed, within a deep old leather hanging bag.
That bag originally landed on me from China.
A gift, not a tourist jab.
Long before, things got sticky over there.
Stuffy nosed lot. spooked us all, by signing red letters again.

All the purest Chinese, ran as fast as their legs could carry them.
The girls with white bandaged feet, who had to play hop scotch.
An old English game, where you jump over squares.
On your feet.
Mustn't touch the lines, or bears come out and eat you.
Children played it on London pavement's streets.
All the paths had squares.
Thinking out loud, as the leather bag stares into my forbidden eyes.

Within its smelly leathery interior.
I found, one pair of black leather sticky boots.
A sole was hanging off one.
Glue unstuck, useless, some shoemakers.

One sole, was about to fall, as was hanging on, like a man hangs onto his wife.
Around the ankle, was a buckle.
Quite neat, plus they're wedges.
You grow a few inches, without wobbling, on stick pin high heeled types.

Another pair, I dug out, was a grey suede set
A zipper on inside.
One zip was stuck.
I remembered the time, I'd chatted about zips with one of my son's.
The Italian one, Italians seem to have good eyes on clothing stuff.
He couldn't work it.
Down to the cobbler, I thought, with my little eye.

Next in line, I found an old pair of sling back high heels.
I stuffed the lot in another bag.
Sainsbury's one, to add to my 'things to do list'.
I felt really chuffed.
I'd finally got stuck into some of my old stuff, I used on wearing feet thing's.
To one of the best shops in town.

'Nicer than Italian ice cream, those old boys 'cobblers '.
You can stand chatting ages, about dimensions with flashy sole extensions.

Don't forget to look after your shoes.
They'll look after your feet.

African Adventures

Seven years seems like seventy
Each crisp breeze was glowing
Singing everything from birds in trees
To lions guarding young cubs on plains in breezes

Beating to a rhythm of a tribal drum
I danced underneath a crying sky
As we chanted our glowing style in feet
Dripping in moonlighting
Under intimacy of tribes wearing
Little other than swinging skirts
Made up of plants beads
As beady blowing glow lit lamps
All went down as the sun goes low

We rattled our cups
A malty red wine brewed as stew smells of aromatic scents expelled
Alongside an African rice hot spicy spread
Along came the moon god
As we all stamped out our other life woes

The Bin Men of Belgravia

I sat breathing in Chelsea air as tears rolled from my eyes full of memoirs.
I'd made it by hook, line and sinker to a midnight dance of Prokofiev's cricket pitched rolling chamber.

Diminuendo was I in buttered flesh.
Spread jam over my green silk lace bodice.
I love being sampled in jam before my blood bath is sprinkled with champagne.
Dancing in strawberry night raindrops of moods in twisting love cups.

A garment tucked away holding the title ' eat me with strawberry jam ".
Counts like red jam, on bread as you know.
Many aperitifs are often dressed with peaches

Floating in thin,
I'd returned to the count of nine pm.
There's no way time baskets weaving on London roads can be controlled.
Parking attendants are henchmen.

Myself having dismounted my white horse-riding North to south overnight.
I dismounted at a small gas station.

By the forest
wearing black fish net stockings.

Only to see a horse maiden wearing cream.
Having galloped the Vale of the White horse down under white horse under Swindon Wiltshire.
I gathered up my black dogs' reigns.
They were as long as his legs with feisty curiosity.

Sherwood forest exploded on me sat nav map.
I'd finally numbered the cell phone drama of three weeks suffering snakes drinking old wine from stale vine leaves into my phone s bedroom.

They're all sitting around their Ouija board, pleading to send me traps to block me from smothering my arms onto the lap of romance

Too bad I nailed my garter belt to post
As bin men of Belgravia whispered local love stories into my morning bread basket.
A croissant with more jam within filled my overnight trunk.
Back-ups are imperative.

Cleopatra Visited

I did a fierce morning sprint.
After drinking expresso wearing pink.
Alongside my velvet cape.
I'm in character as a fifteenth century Norse code aunt.
I spilt a tub of black ink, over my breakfast burrito sandwich.
All lying on a broken piece of paper.
Still wearing pink.

I was stitching by nightfall,
for cheers to souvenirs.
Adapting linen from a fashion show,
where I was once hidden.

Behind red drapes,
like a glowing wizard's dwarf on tap,
but in a magical trap.
Also stitching capes for long legged queens, walking with snakes
round their stockings.
In shoes that are wedged with silk seams.
The additional snakes clasp into gold buckles.
These were actually crafted in-bed,
On a midsummers night's dream.

Don't ask the price?
Unless, you want a cat kiss.
They're my-craft,
I stitched together, by lack of gold to go down the Spanish steps in

Rome.
One of my other favourite holes.
Those Italians at it again.
Hasta la Vista!
A Spanish tongue twister.

Took three dogs today
down under a dark bridge.
Underneath suicide hot spots,
where I've saved a few sinners,
from tipping over the edge.

Incidentally during my spiritual memoirs of giving kisses of life after death.
Cleopatra herself arose, patted me on the head.
On my muddy steps walking,
whilst doggie tails wagged alongside, as spooky whales hung out snorting.

Ticking me off.
Cleopatra called me.
I hurled her up out the bloody Thames mud bath
Carried her home.
Now she's sitting on her new throne
In my apartment block one hundred and nineteen
A century whereupon Egyptian Queen landed
To meet with Moi.
I was half so chuffed, now I'm back in my pink dream.

Dead Men's Corpses

The stink of decaying carcases drift from abandoned boats
intermixing alongside London Thames River mud, where blood
baths rise or fall with the changing tides.

A stench so profound one hangs onto one's golden slippers,
becoming drenched within sands from executions of such
disdainful brands.
Upon ports tied up to times
A needle with a dried-out thread,
which can no longer find its eye anymore.
A bony line of battered boats eyes wink directly into my eyes.
Beckoning my flesh to come hither hither
Like a poisonous invisible branch sticking out of this river,
towards me within the rising mist.
On this cloudy London morning.

My men in bed still snoring.
Rosy cheeked fresh young sons.
Having no inkling thought other than what's going on within
that other world.
One of robots on their way soon, so I'm told.

Yet, I the poor poet never many pennies in my purse.
They pour in from an invisible pen.
A rehearsal of life I once rehearsed

Royalties landing have no cave to see through.
For present dragons running our land.
Suck everything out.
That old bloke the taxman with yellow stockings worn high above his toes,
has his claws out and about without any concerns.
What's?
much on your toes...
yet his stockings much longer than his nose.

Melted thoughts sweeping through me.
While the battered boats still winking.
A blindness into history.
Trying to lure me into its den.
I stand, staring.
Curiosity overrides as my imagination bears a beat.
One would not swim with decayed corpses.
Seals now joined the herd.
They have some inside this river cocktail I'm told.
Seabass fish too swim here now.
Fisherman catch them for dinner.
Madness if you ask me.
Yet, the river cleans itself from life's dirty laundry.
Sometimes one thinks one's on the French Riviera.
The boats of the dead lined up for my inspection.

My black dog Bingo the lion heart has more intent to catch ducks now paddling in packs.
He licks his hanging tongue.
His gliding eyes ride ripples inside the water.

Working out how to grab his fresh breakfast.
A duck breakfast on the beach yummy he surveys the
surrounding street.
Checking on security.
The other dead men walking.
I doubt our local security would blink one eye.
Half asleep on the beat.
Usually drunk on other herbs too.
Useless security in this neck of the woods.
Get your own invisible gun.
Or the ghosts will get you to sink with t'others.

We step forth for two dark figures stroll towards us in this hole.
The lights gone down.
As if the dead boats chanted a spiritual call.
Waking the dead to help mend their body battered from
neglectful drunken sailors.
Now dead inside the riverbed nesting inside
this wet graveyard.
We must stand my black dog with I to attention,
as two darkened bodies rise up from the sand.
Maybe we've wakened the dead after all.

The Man with the Bloody Hands

A dramatic start began as I opened my Saturday morning gatehouse gate.

At my gate, it's cast-iron steel now.
I've made my year two thousand plus thirty/ two.
I decided to jump ten years in my home-made time machine.
All because I dislike wars.

My new security belt is somewhat futuristic.
I've even employed a robot called Stew.

Turning wooden planks into steel thumps
I blew out a spraying spell.
Created by my recently blister filled
binding white fleshy hands
On adding a touch of French water
I sat sipping my South African morning brew.

A man with blood dripping from his right hand arrived at my gate.
He wasn't a stranger; we'd crossed paths before.
His dog befriended mine a few weeks in time
Upon dog swimming in line with big tides.
Deep inside Londoners riverside sinking mud.

Sometimes on a good day
golden brown sand lights up
the playground slides nearby.

Young children sing upon.
Over by t'other side of the bank.
You can just about spot them
Don't try to dot to dot them.
Your pencil will go blunt in trying to catch them
In their sliding rhythm.

Here say, I say.
I witnessed fresh blood at my gate.
Crack of dawn it was so.
I was wringing wet
I've got a Chinese laundrette paraphernalia process
It's all going on today
between my gatehouse
my laundries hanging dripping wet,
reaching right up to second floors
indoors inside going up my stairs.

Lo and behold a blood soaking man
Hailing his dripping red wet right hand
up high in the air!
Begging he pleaded 'please Mademoiselle',
'Let me into your house'.

As said, I knew the gent in question.
Bloodshed is quite up my own path
I hasten to bring to your attention.
Be it one of my genes
be an offset from a post-war nurse.

My Celtic grandmother set a medical clinic up, up town not down.
Therefore, I immediately put my blue nurse apron strings on.
Hauled the gentleman indoors.

On patching his dripping bloodshed up
as I untied my first aid kit.
My new robot Stew who's just arrived
He whizzed off to discuss my exciting news of the day.

Stew my robot gave me a beady eye wink.
Now my laundries back in my sink.
The man has a clean hand.
So now as I smile it's back to sucking pen time.
I must not forget about my now
most unfortunately
Icy tea.

I vow to carry on
Stew needs my mind
Hand in hand.

Spiritual Intoxication

Holding a creative spear.
A team of lions await
The producer. at his north London gate.
isn't there anything he can't create?

I'm sitting on my rusty throne
remembering my labour drone
A tired midwife's hands pulled, as I pushed.
I screamed from 'A Royal Free pharmaceutical confectionery '.
A north London hub.
Opening to one hundred - sixty degrees.
I cannot label by kings who execute fair maidens,
in the wings.
For hearts as pure as silk,
don't require much mothers nursing numbers.
Simmering, as is, my out of tank breast milk.
His hungry tongue, lay routes down.
Then became quite an impertinent maestro.
Rising to a wolf that sighed
On crawling out his cradle
My first instinct was to fetch stickers,
to bang upon a garden gated piano.
I'd labelled.
Hands on.

My desk creaks
In disbelief, I weep,

Which often sends my weary eyes.
off to grab a little sleep.

On waking from lands,
within other dimensions
Leading to joyful frames, as thus above.
I stir my English tea with three spoons of sugar.
My blood is very boring
' A positively '.
it should be way up over my head times three!

A Red Bicycle Stand

My black wolf picked up a dead man's scent.

I was led to the crime scene

On the riverbed, where dead men's smells filtered out from dirty underwater sirens bleeping with riverbeds stinking dirty laundry.
Unwashed for months
He'd left his wallet full of credit cards and cash
On the handle bar of his bike.
Tied up to his red bike handles.
He'd chucked his boots on the side
Letters were rolled up within
Me being the saintly poet on route
Fetched his dirty black boots
They still stink now
I unrolled evidence of his sins
I've handed the muddy wallet loaded with cash into the local cops down under within t'other floors..

Incidentally he' was a gangster on the run
Too much for the sinners' dinners to greet within shark's jaws where I sit pondering

I've unwrapped paper tied up in smelly socks
I've got the phone numbers in Italy to unroll a plot
What's my next stop?
I'm brewing coffee on the rocks

Adding fire crackers on the top
A frothy spelling curse adds a bit more alphabetical cream on top
A dead man's flesh was gone
It's wrapped up in water weeds now

On visiting London crime lords
The dude got nailed
He got his stomach lining filled up
Easy does it, easily down this end of town
Usually an innocent bypassing stranger
would have nicked the cash
Then hung it, as guilt wears no complex in some Tongues can't lie, they get goosebumps
weight of tastebuds that switch off around the bent clock in time lords time wharfs wings.

If red eyes devour their guilty minds
Let red tongues sing as having been hung talking of me
Those hanging from his stinking socks are as frail as my own purse
What the hell
I'll live on green tea and write verse
So I starve on honestly
Awaiting my pay check
Then I'll rock the house down

Having hung himself right round the back of my back door
My eyes rise up like the sand over the dead on my floor
I surmise I've been dragged into waves

upon the next tidal wave
I waved farewell

My wolf picked up the scent distinctly
one hour too late for my next page turner

I'm set to save a corpse now gone to rest where sharks get laid on their evening song bed

Dolls News

I'm overwhelmed we suddenly have a leader with some noodles
I'm nearly laughing to the bank
Although mines an empty think tank
It won't be for long

The Red on the left twiddles their thumbs in gritty grottoes
Look through the eye of the needle
As great minds unwind their thread

It's plain as blinking daylight
The groovy blonde new MP
Has nearly as many noodles as me
No, we don't eat the Chinese
Neither at Won Tong land
Scatter your beans down China Town
Off the back streets of soho
Do a 180-degree spin on your dancing feet
Don't run noses with the laughing beggar
He's laughing his socks off
Be it their smelly, underneath his wellington's.
His feet I mean.

Ring the bell number ten I'm ecstatic with adrenaline
Running through my ultra blue veins
Not my hair.

In swings and roundabouts
Politics does a twist
The blue party are back at top of Dolly's charts
You see, by lifting taxation
Everyone's going to come dancing in London
Even the mean bankers in NYC
London is singing in the rain
I'm going to launch my next blue band
The jam is on
My fingers are pattering on top of my head

The Crazy High Five

Give us a five!
They're all alive
No bundles from my tummy got off without
Inhaling some pure Doll drug

My late grandmother said
"T's all in the breeding ".
Well, mine was a banana split cocktail
Added to a mixture of vodka from polish quarters
With Scottish haggis
Bonne appetite
I can't place the French exclamation mark
Onto an English iPhone
It just about copes with my illiteracy
Give the dog a bone
A touch of tongue in cheek humour
Can only go down my "Asphodelus" tube philosophically
speaking

Bite your tongue deliberately
Or accidentally on purpose
Apparently dinosaurs' urine
Makes up half our earths water
T's another BBC gift of a stout journalists got smacked jargon
On the five am show

Don't watch the box
Radio 4 won't makeshift your snoring.

Back-to-back bench
I'm giving you a helping hand
In dissection of my clan
Displayed in black, white Fontaine pentameters

It was a box shot on a dark subway
Metro the title in gay Paris
The underground tube in London the city of the dead
Who's who?
If you work this puzzle out
You're a master of indigoes
I'm as baffled as you

I might tip you off at the next stop ⬢

Modern Day Paraphernalia

I'm still alive and kicking folks.
I had a shark attack in block number ten.
January twenty-three was bound to begin with a shark's jaws.
Bitingly swift
You get the drift?
My Wi-Fi was bugged
I guess it's those spiders again.

Fortunately, I clamped an ant attack
Fast as my ten fingers could play the darn number ten fiddle
I may as well get on the blinking roof.
Like the musical, and sing!
' If I were a rich man '

Ants were the aftermath, of my teenage chef's indulgence within
playing chef of many different experimental styles of cuisine.
He'd scarpered to Scarborough
Not the fairground.
He's twiddling his thumbs underneath aeroplanes now.
Mum gets lumbered with all their dirty laundry too
To add to this last domestic nightmare
I was attacked by mice too
These two teenagers with hormones sizzling
Well one of them now overdosed on a Swedish woman
Left mummy (me) with full camping gear
Old sausages leftover from camping experiences
The mice did doth have one hell of a midnight feast.

Back to now. My fingers are still green.
The sun is shining
I'm trying to get the blasted Wi-Fi figured out
My teenage dream ain't been nothing other than a nightmare off street Elm
Not like that screen number.

I'm going off to serve hot toast with scrambled eggs a la carte.
I've just hitched a job as a waitress on wheels!
Thank the lord.
Although, my usual daily scream of words is
'Lord have mercy! '
I got a broken dish washer to top the load.

I've had some blinking issues in house
As you might gather.
I've nailed a London theatre down
I'll keep you guessing

January 11 / 2023

Invisible Servant

Dust mixed up with dog's smells.
With the cat upstairs in the penthouse.

Somethings a bit twisted in my household.
How come I end up being the servant?
While the others all swept away to hide on higher quarters.
Like the blinking Ritz Hotel in this place.
The way my son's ride their golden horse driven carriages by midnight to another side of town.
Escape while we have the chance!
mother's out with her household broom.
Before we have to clean.
Do a runner.
Mother looks very meaningful
Leaving mother dear in the peaceful whispering night air.
Just a mop, a boom.
A desk full of bill's.
Holding onto my cash bucket in today's moon.

Rising higher than my highest high healed suede burgundy boots.
Spotted then yesterday in the midst of digging through my over filled closet.
I've had to hitch a few more pitches.
My wardrobe seems to have grown.
Now I pinched my waist in to size twenty four inches.
Another two I will wear one of those Victorian corsets without screaming when my invisible maid pulls in the laces.

Agent au Provocateur.
Name of the brand.
Not dirt cheap.
Modelling day's rolling in the sand.
One or two number's roll in.
Then it's casting ditches.
Bye bye.

Had to scream through a few Sunday preaches.
Never made it to church, so the pastor is going to sing notes of discarded untuned chords while I kneel on the steps of the cathedral with my sins lying down.
How many do I have? Sins?
Oh lot's I never got to where I am without being nailed in a pot.

Warning the next draft we ride
it's full of mud in sweaty dripping mouths.

Ducks Quacking Quack Quack

Meetings upon life moments.
A friendly duck went quack, quack. quack.
Then turned around and bit my head off.
I wear it well, as it's hanging on.

One duck wore feathers,
at an English meeting of liquorice all sorts.
On a fine June day in West Sussex England.

One duck quacked a quack my way full of false pretences.
Offered me a duck's breast.
With sauce too.
Not the Chinese brand.
A northern English quartet that played the harp off-key.
That duck laid out his jam of fake strawberries.

In the meantime, inside another false tavern.
Another northern nest.
The southern part of town rings ding dong bells on pound notes.
Lined up at his gate was a blonde skinny bird.
The kind my other half then hates.
No bottoms no teeth worth paying for to munch.
I was invited there once to tea time.
Whereupon my other -half then, had just bitten my bottom.
Half were expensive to line his teeth.

She holds her feathers on.
The skinny northern tart, who's blonde.
False blonde streaks lie down to her skinny hips.
One female duck goes along with the show.
Have a halfway house fancy nest.
Her pouch is full.
Is all that matters to some in life.
The size of a male duck's wallet.

Ducks are often wives in disguise,
Easier to pluck.
You know all about those feathered kinds of birds.

On gathering my tired wings,
after my mother duck dropped dead.
One Christmas afternoon.
She flew off to gates where the angels wait.
Don't blame her do you?

I flew up to northern hills.
I had a fat man's ducks phone number, hidden in-between my breasts.
My legs were pretty long.
No meat under my flesh.

My band and I were hopping ducks.
We consisted of an Aston Martin kind of brand.
A creature out of nowhere appeared wearing a double-coated caramel white fur coat.

Big-ears hung down, with a fiercely pointed nose.
Also possessing nasal buds to sniff out a crack dealer a mile off.

I filled up my Aston Martin.
My spy wagon.
All under-cover.
Lent to me by one spy who worked for the cops.
Had a get-out-of-jail-free card.
tried to get inside my knickers.
Send him running.
I quacked as I hopped hopscotch.
You remember the name of the game.

On my introduction to a dark hairy duck upon resting my head.
I sat on the wing of a white swan.
White swan introduced me to another bird.
A wild sorcerer, she had silver hair.
She told me and the black dog wouldn't half get along.

Disguised well with James Bond animalistic covers of down under.
I allowed my thoughts to reap the benefits beyond a reasonable doubt,
I'm now a loaded white-feathered swan.
Spartan, the beast thinks he's boss right now.
Doing time around the clock.

I think, as I quack, quack to my t'other ducks.
Hanging my wet pants up on the t'other side of my northern nest.
The city grins at us birds.

We beat down ducks who snarled but can't quack.
As a matter of fact.

Ducks sit staring on my window ledge,
are from a ghost's heyday.
A haunted house inn, rests in a northern valley, has some awesome bending dark alleys.

Nineteen- sixty -nine.
Might have been my dead mother's nest.
Our heydays were never really of the Bond Street London scene.

Good evening I'm out on the town now are you too?
Grab a northern beer say cheers.
Quack, quack.
Where art though now?

I think we are all in the year two thousand and twenty-two.
The year we all went around the bend then reversed to two thousand and twenty-two.
The Charleston quack may have flappers on their wings too.

Climate Sums Three Men French Kissing

Oh, dearie me what a pity.
Monsieur Macron had to sum up his man at the top to a
Glaswegian hop stop.
He's taking a plane to Edinburgh in a hurry.
I surmise Charles De Gaul airport in romantic Paris, be his take-off point.

T's all truly frantic for the Brits went to block a French vessel.
In the middle of President Macrons' kissing program.
He had to slip into view the dilemma,
Be it French kissing is more important than fish.
One cannot market French wine without the spread.
Scottish waters still have ultimately the best quarters of pink fish.
Damn the pink champagne!
The poet had hers nicked at a disastrous summer supposedly romantic party.
Tut, tut, tut. I get no French kisses anymore.
My old lover man's tongue has been doing tongue twisters.

Blowing farts through balloons is more erotic.
If you never tried its such fun.

Back to plain sailing.
Joan Crawford has come up from the dead.
Given me a few tips on how to get wed.

President Macron has returned to his long French kiss.
The men in skirts at my end of the globe.
They're all lined up with whiskey and haggis on the stove.
Got to get you French toads pissed.
You might sign a deal then.
Our Scottish belles will outdo your romantic French duets.
I heard threesomes are on your betting card.
Be it I'm a half Scots lass, you may well, or may not know!

Have a bonnie time, we Scots are too sharp to fall for snails.
Unless you charm us under our coat and tails.

Auld Lang's Syne

In The Evening Light

I'm sitting on a dark wooden chair was once a weapon for hypnotising customers in exotic artistic tanks

A tightly dressed apron thrilled white frilly black short skirt high heeled female fatale.

Make those heels black said her boss.

Patent will act as one's tool to seduce
artistically inclined minds hanging out of coffee cups drooling over my arty pieces.

T'was an art cafe in heyday moments hanging
In dreamland.

Two thousand and twelve I sucked myself under tables with legs that twisted round and around.
Those waitresses with small hips,
as mine are now, wore thickened brimmed spy glasses.

In the evening light sitting over London Bridge.
One reminisces on many a pound buster.
That was dragged to the floor.
Jealous scoundrels
till the cake bakes.
London lights.
City nights.
One wonders where I will be tomorrow.

We're not living in the moonlight now.

A Man in Green Velvet

He stood unannounced,
outside a smart looking place roundabout my end of town.
His green attire caught my stare
A poetic eye is always on alert,
for life's hidden treasures
Yet, often quite unaware,
to what we're sucking under our thickened city skin.

As all the London characters expose their insides come pouring
out, right up to tips of noses or eyebrows firm, but bold.
By what they wear, or how they tilt a brolly, into the London air.
Or, hold their hat
It's a matter of fact.

So there he stood awaiting, glaring at a street premises
Unaware my artistic needle had pinned him down already.
Seeing eye to eye.
I'm envisaging weary waving images
floating through my busy mind.

Politely, I approached, seeking his consent to shoot a short shot
My veins tremble upon these kind of folk
who make me choke with underestimated pins and needles.

I'd caught another yolk, fresh from a free bird's nest
Thought I, through my little third eye
Upon my scattering my request

He instantly replied, standing upright both his feet still on the ground.
I'm wondering, if he had high wedges on, indeed.
He suddenly grew in size.
Be it, underneath long velvet pantaloons
Not British Tweed.
I might well heed to your attention.

Perhaps he's born from an India tribal hierarchy
His Indian mannerism was astoundingly precise
Forget turmeric on rice.
This gentleman obviously knew his game on London business terrain
His tunes up the right street, even if he sings from Indian bellies.

Well, you see. One, two, three's a number for me
Unfortunately, many boutiques plus avenues with plenty of spice.
Have closed down
Everyone's broke
Except the richest sheiks,
left holding hot plates watching the English bellies grow fat.

Three Thousand More Miles

We Three Kings of Orient Are
We ride through the night under holy light.
God directs the route.

Riding over sandmen's graves.
Our camels know the right pathway.
Be it dark but light shines through upon us.

Our sacks are full of many golden pieces.
A market gathering awaits us serving hot mulled wine.
Binding time under stars.
Our stomachs rumble that help us solider on.

Many beggars will await at that market gate.
Not so far away.
Only three hundred miles more.

We will but deplore to look after all those beggars.
Hungry for some wine with scones.
We're sure to have some left for the poor.
They be as needy to fill their empty stomachs.
Then the gates to Jerusalem will open.
So be our destiny, whereby lies our fate.

Our rich associates doth await.
Handing us with more gold coins to have and to hold.

Now hear us people loud and clear.
We are but tired merchants,
Please lend your ears to our stories.
Three hundred miles more.
Come meet us at the market stalls.

Our camels may then drink holy water,
Refilling their natural tank.
May we permit our noble beasts to take a rest.
Two weeks in Jerusalem to feast, drink, sell out wares and be merry.

We're then all set for we will be spilling with gold.
As the rich unfold gifts from our many journeys.
Upon which we collected much.
We will eat, drink and be merry.

The poor will crawl as usual around back doors.
Life is never a fair spread, but our good Lord sees all.

Have mercy on those rich greedy souls we sell golf to.
We need to all drink too.

God rest ye merry gentleman.

Everything Washed Out

My washing machine is once again spinning
Rather than leaking.
A man with a bag turned up from a back street
An engineer of sorts
Our eyes bleeped long and hard.

I offered him a cup of tea
He turned it down, but got down on his knees.
Twisting knobs we're his forte
Unlike my tired screwdrivers hand.

I got no Italian son around my bend in the road
After getting laid
I under-covered a crime scene
My kids were never going to be normal produce.

I'm glad they're not, but I did cherish a handyman son.
He's zipped off to my private jet captains pitch.
The plane is stranded in a Yorkshire ditch.
My cars been off parole
London is too damn costly to maintain wheels
I just about survive in my expensive high heels
Twenty quid for heeling tips.
They're a stiletto brand high end.
Burgundy snake skin inspired.
Not sure what my neighbours think of my new attire.
Going blonde bombshell meant change of pace

I might go flying
At least the old machine is now spinning my briefs of best lace.
They're from Paris
The best lingerie normally is.

Another day in shivering loneliness
but dogs create great ladders in my back black seams.
I'm in fifteenth century England now
Not sure if stilettos were in then?
Doubt it.
More a wedge hammer to cut off some heads.

Tips To Conservatives Heading For PM

Watch out folks
It be a mighty sin to step into the shoes of losers
Unless you got your pound note sticking on your crown
Don't be a jerk like the last dope
Mayor of eccentricity is one thing
An over bleached balding head with a fat belly not flat belly
You stupid piggies in the middle
Go get drunk when you finished your business
If it's dirt under the tablecloth
Don't hide your noses from each other's private affairs
Dig out the dirt
Vomit it up all over the lace white tablecloth
William Churchill held his whiskey enough to grind minds underneath the trenches
Those were men who could behave well while knocking back till the drop
Gone are men of skinless stomach
propaganda nowadays rides like the Queen of England
You can't breathe if you got skeletons hiding in your closet
So only ride the role to MP fame if you don't wear Dolly Parton's knickers like you did last night in the end game.

Remember rules are made to be broken
Therefore make sure you lay down the best ones.
Break a leg
As always show business is the best business

Bells In the Night Air

Bells went off in the midnight hour.
Not once, not twice. Four times in the depths of haunting hour.
A man carrying an electric cannister filled with wining steel worms.
Repaired mothers house bells.
They went off-pitch, in mothers house, after he slid his worms out.
Sitting on a northern hilltop, by a stinging blueberry bush ditch guarded by stinging nettles.
Here I am.
Alone with a black dog and a cheeky pug.

At the end of my patience, I collapsed with mothers ghost, on my grannies green velvet couch.
Then, I plastered my worn out face with anti-aging cream.
A Swiss brand consisting of gel-like beans,
which pop full of purple texture gel, which explodes into a sticky glue type liquid.
Lifts one's face to age twenty two without going under the surgeon's knife.
The black dog stared at me as though I was stark raving mad.
I am, of course, but let's keep that a secret between me and you.
'The anti -aging bombshells'.
The tube is blonde, in any event, nested.
Hanging, from a bag of hundred and two handbags staring at me off broken shelves.
In the morning light I awoke rested inside deep velvet with young

skin.

The only thing to conquer now was how to gain enthusiasm to win the next problem.

Life throws us down drains more times than the old piano standing in the hall reminisces of when it was last played by my mother a real pianist.

I played my first tune on too.
Now it's all mine and ' My old piano is crying too'

A Midnight Chase

The night air shone
I was down in the beach running three dogs
One is s hound with a nose as strong as the Big Ben clock.
Time was ticking, but the tide was high as the waves crashed on in.
Was the weekend rolling aftermath of many a drinking sprawl.
The hung over people were floating by us
Avoiding our long hound noses
Probably carrying weed to try clear out evil fluid intoxications.
Or crack cocaine to run through the dark hung over corpses
Plenty dead men resurfaced
From down under the tides screams.
Saturday night a point for local residents to do the big jump
Off into no man's land.
There's sharks here sometimes now.
They've been cleaning up the bones.

In midst of our midnight meditation
A man way out of his mind came running towards me
Screaming out 'I'm gonna kill you lady '.
My dogs caught the drift of this threatening creature
We turned by a quick number
I was most fortunately wearing flats.
We ran as fast as we could towards my house
Slammed my door shut
With one mighty bang.
Phoned the cops

Did they turn up?
Heavens no

The rest of this story must wait for after dinner
So grab your glass of rum, vodka or simply martini
Or if you're truly holy
Perhaps simply water.

A Parade of Dolls Enemies

Be it heard a mystic of international applause
Says tut, tut.
We know who you are.
Inspector Graham might be down on the farm
Yet, an old Druid's arm, gave him a tip.
Whilst tethering mud off his sheep.

A man with a long beard, grey haired
Rather balding but hairs hanging on.
His name be too unearthly for me to scribble
He pulled up his truck
Full of feed for animal's jaws lay open
Begging for more.
The two country men plucked ideas outside an old barn

Spiritual whispers floated from countryside's hills
Down under to where I currently sit herewith
Having just licked my lips on a tasty plate of fish.
Caught at five am.
Am old rod still had a hook an eye left
Off I went.
Over by the other side.
Kent's rivers filled upon thunderstorms rain belts overflowing yesterday
Luckily for me.

Spiritual ghouls arose carrying woven baskets
They were filled with herbs.
Messages echoed from plants, whilst chanting
Plants reinforced their position
Making it a mission.
Not an impossible transition
Plants communications
Be vividly honest with purity.
Beyond the end of my line.
Dewey mist overhung overhead.

Upon gathering these mystical messages
Much has come clean.
Even though I'm about to glide upon low tide waves with my creatures.
They're awaiting at my gate.
I'm to run to the shoreline now.
Are you coming with me?

January 4/2023

Personally French

Thinking with the French snails
T's pretty clear you have the devil in your tube
The metro downstairs was a map of paraphernalia.
Yet, I lived in a Parisian Street, so had to get my antenna out.

Now, look here you devils snails.
Have you forgotten your garlic?
T's openly obvious you have no garlic left
It's gotten beyond the pale of the whales whining around waters
trying to survive from fishermen hurling nets.
Or be it the salmon queen.

I'm saddened your land was once a place I played my bass guitar.
Forcing evil won't get you out the dung you yourself macron
serviettes sewn by self-inflicted ugly stitches.

I don't see how a land of holiness, be it hiding now
One which has many a fine priest executed of recent herrings you
caught off English white cliffs.

I have to discuss this at the stones.
A highly spiritual tomb I will but weep upon tonight.
later by nightfall when black ravens fly.

I shall mark my order after my holiness wipes his forehead in
dissatisfaction of you bending Napoleons law backward.

I have but a mighty tomb in Paris to suck out time.
Time-beds from some wicked men owe me some favours.

I did but meet my wizard there upon Parisian streets.
We had a coffee disgusting what's up the next street now get your fresh garlic in a hurry.
I don't want to eat you fresh in the flesh.

A Ritzy Affair With My Dwarf

One fine sunny summer London afternoon.
I was invited for lunch at 'The Ritz ', by my favourite dwarf.
Being more specific,
at times he's been quite horrific towards my hair.

He smokes a pipe, this particular dwarf.
Forgets his chewing gum lying hidden,
inside his back blue coat loaded with Erin- moor.
A brand that these tiny men adore
For it allowed him to feel taller on way to top floors.

Half stinks the house down with all the smoke.
A brand that still stands at James's Tobacco boutique by the sunny side of the London strand.

He'd lost all his legal cases up to now,
so despicably.
That, my blue flowing hair distracted the likes of the wicked.

The grey mops on top of the addressed lady
I configure;
Her boss a big timer in both fields
' women versus gambling affairs'.

Fluttering through my mind,
like men being slaughtered in a casino.

An elderly stale secretary,
quite high end,
sat upon my round table at t'other end.
Leaving me floating at t'other corner
Josephine her name.

I was just arm candy back then
To an exclusive lawyer on a client's pitchfork!

I was pulled around like a casino's waitress-with yellow long legs.,

So, going out with a dwarf was interesting
If I've hitched you in a pitch.
Come back soon for part two.
Imagine what romance sprung up from dining with my dwarf?
Behind sitting 'At the Ritz', as the arm candy Queen
Being torn to pieces?
I've now got an itch, have to scratch fast, before another riddling affair comes around.

Doggie Bag Tails

I stood outside in bright winter sunshine
A trail of blue bags flew out of my coat pocket.
Doggie bags clutching within my garments
Got dragged out into morning sunlight
By a brisk tail end, of a northern singing wind stream.

Blue bags wrapped around my green coated legs
Some old slacks I'd bunged on in haste to pick up my morning aphrodisiac
' Cappuccino ', on the rocks of the River Thames
Could be a worse way to start the day.
Maybe I'm a blue leftover Christmas cracker.
I wonder who'll win my present within?

The Wife's Secrets

The brown faced girl told me it all
You thought she was your trusted friend
She has it all inside her Jamaican mystic ball
On lying through her woven hair,
which strung out lies on tambourine drums.

Bang, she dragged you over to a Ochio Rio's Jamaica plantation
Fed you grapes as she picked bones on me
Not to mention!

The blonde-haired playboy man was your best friend
He left her covered within golden sandy beaches
Madam two faced stuck her claws into you and me
Laid down her bargain on your table, like burnt crusty bread.
Now, she's waiting to steal you away to her parlour
Not too far away from your bend in Kingston harbour
She's laying in gold with her lying black board sketched,
all ready for her next game of chess

Mr playboy club is sitting in millionaires row downstairs
He took the fast train on Miami Beach
Earn a dime he said, as he's biting his nails now
Smarty pants breathed hurricanes out in shock horror
At how you screwed up
Believing his old woman he left breathing out all your dead wife's
secrets to your real-life mistress
Be wise who one trusts!

A Grey-Haired Ghost

Upon walking upon muddy riverbeds
My boots sank down saturating their rubber soles in mud
The tide was low, as the evening light dipped depicting a
crimson glow upon waving movements of tidal transitions

I'd been hailed to hoist up masts
A dead sailor girl with short sleek back and sides
Conversation with ghosts is highly deplorable

I zipped up a tatty diving suit darn quick
My own tavern is busting at the seams
it's overspill in boarding tickets
make any other adventurous spirit breath sighs of relief they're
not in my shoes.

I've done enough bleeding weeping the last week to soak into
baths with natural sea salt
They say it's good for our skin

weeping mermaids configure they can't line up in Queens lines
My tail is rather complex
I'm looking after Thames river ghosts instead

Well in all good effect
Sound crew now please!
" Action'!
Our Queen ensembles with the dead
Be it her post be of supernatural monarchical strength to seventh

heaven we point our compass
Sitting with ghosts by masts

I held my own conversations with London ghosts
Hooked on line by the zipping wet suit
An auction which was dirt cheap
deep diving never comes cheap

Upon an old dead woman's yacht
Be it, it's cloaked in rattling canisters
One has to carry back up even if one's dead at sea or on land
I had a great conversation with a grey haired sea ghost
There's the next in line our new king to sip red wine with
God save the King
I wonder why mermaids need diving suits?

In The Midnight Air

Oh how I screamed with vulgarity
When a demon spit at me
Before the clock struck twelve earlier on
Letting out internal pain
The demons cannot catch me now
Sometimes they sniff around trying to pull my hair

Do you remember those wicked schoolgirls who pulled your hair?
Usually when your teachers back was turned.
Well pull all you want you decayed slob.
You can't pull it out.
It's not a wig like your oyster you eat in the champagne bar.
Eat, eat your smelly feet.

I don't think those who wear wigs would hide under your coat
tails in even with dripping oysters they give off.

You used to push buttons
Whet a snob
They're all flat in that hat.
The cats whiskers have a better effect licking my bust blister.

Who is crying now?
Go on ask the pilot to burn all those love letters from years ago.
I think your best dress stinks to muddy town bars.
Where local tramps sit begging.
Not that, they tramp you screwed around the cherry hill will let

you free
She's sending you to the third realm to fit on her knee.
Old baked tarts will be hovering like hungry cows.
Moo, moo.

God will not give lemons five minutes, so don't knock on his gate now.

The Dumping Ground Of Bird C

The mysterious dumping ground for the second round to be chosen to dump the birdie.
A sour cherry pie, that although sour to the taste has a golf course around the bend.

There seems to a strange convention being aligned.
In a male riddle with a male beast who dances small circles around his new female band will be lined up by the south side of the beach.

The new agenda stepping forth soon in a meeting on the cards at a northern Carolina room is splendorous naked drool.
.
The long-legged lady in the brown skirt knows all
No one is been straight to the man with the pipe.
Miss Cherrie is aiming to return, but you are only one of her bands. She has three.
All on island.
You are too desperate for love from any kind of flying bird to see

An Evil Practice

Don't think I'm blind to foolish practises.
I entered your twenty -four hour practise just t'other day.
My black dog sniffed out your corruption the moment I stepped in the door.
For he was trained with myself with fine Christian dog scholars.
We were taught how to hunt down morons a mile off.
Oh, you the evil silver-haired un-Christian female.
The one sitting on the front desk, while a badly bleached blonde man did somersaults of grief on your badly printed dance floor that holds no truth
For on that freezing November morning, you saw me coming
I might look loaded with pound notes dear reception.
Sadly I had to bend over many wine bottles ; for years of my loyalty to a wealthy hypocritical liar.
Who smoked a pipe as he laid out a whole bucket full of promises.
Are my youth while putting that pipe.
As my secretary mentioned on the phone.
The lady at part Ms Melech never skips an appointment regarding her animal flock.
Therefore the September date is of fraudulent corruption, or either I a secretary to the dear lady Madam Melech, I should say.
Tut tut naughty haughty taking extra money from her indeed.
This note herewith might or might not be up to your own translation, for it be clear your practice needs a slap on the face.
In journalistic style this write I will succumb to bear a translation in later hours of the day.

Upsetting poets isn't a wise move.
Thank you to those who upset me.
I now have mountains of stories to sell.

Good morning to the creeps who tried to seduce me with false pennies who failed
Your balls are empty Sir now

Princess Ukraine

I met them for the first time
They are as sweet as strawberries
You could add champagne
I bought one bottle of snap crackle pop!
We never opened the bubbly stuff.
I was going onward behind car's wheels
A dark long dusty drive wearing rock 'n-roll gear
Handling dogs alongside my angel sent wheels
A car in a dream, all because of a Blackheath witch.
You may recall my screaming sprawl
As I set feet down to hit the dirt road north.
I'm back in another smelly city.
This time is like no other moment in a time warp
I stopped on route, boy did I hoot my horn whilst playing my tambourine.
I've met my Ukrainian princesses.
How joy beholds in English shores
'Twas an afternoon of " lions- maid" ice cream
I'm fasting, work that one and you're the next contestant of Ukrainian beauty magazine
The kings and queens comp on the miss world stomping stop .
All hail!
England's smiling again

The Grey-Haired Ghost (2)

Now when I walk alongside the riverbed
Seeing abandoned yachts tied up
Often with movement down under from cabins within
Even a flashlight sparkles sometimes
I stop to wink while I do a double whammy thinking
Underneath my wild hair bush
Cut short by scissors that belong to me
Not to Edward, his hair is off the top of...
Of Miami Vice on fast cars with out of reach cops

Chopped the blinking lot
In one go
Couldn't have Bob Marley's Look
Dreadlocks not my thing
Rag Dolls hair is like Liza Minnelli's now
Thank God it's not short on top
It'll grow alongside the way I walk the rising tide
My cheeks are bright pink blushing at Ghosts
Seems to real the dead in

She's invited me for another blinking British cuppa
Mrs Ghost
Crack of dawn on her noisy yacht
I know she's dead but it doesn't bother me
I watched her vanish before my black dog's eyes
Into the sea

The American Presidents in town
He might rub noses with our new female Prime M

The Hand with A Green Fly

In the summer heat in London Town
An unusual species of blood sad sucking mosquitoes
Appeared with extended fangs
They cling onto your flesh biting down underneath
Oxygenated cells screaming
Leaving exterminated red swollen goosebumps
A milky fluid erupts as their bite gets a grip

An aftermath of serious itching
Be it a red sticky tapeworm fighting to breath
Appears on a sidewalk
Of your ankles

No it's not the monkeys swinging
On oak trees.
The viruses from them
Are hanging on only promiscuous fleshy humans
Those who don't keep zips up on pants.

These beastly flies
Are new on the block.
I've hung long brown misquote fly tape up
Now that brown tape will murder those creatures

Animal worshippers
don't want our own flock penetrated
By slimy venomous frogs.

Neither, do we intend to worship
Caviar or French snails without
Garlic tails.

An evening sunset now sets in
As tropical living in London
Is becoming a sin we now ride with.

A Lonely Piano

A piano sits, crying all alone
Wondering why?
It's been left abandoned
With no one to play him

Covered in a dark blue felty textured quilt
Underneath are pure ivory keys
Elephants tusks, were considered money pots.
As everything beautiful is tormented

The finest fingers in the land
Used to play concert pieces rituals
Her names my Mother Anne
Now playing in heaven's corridors for Bogdan
My father, her one and only man
He's holding his paintbrush

I grew up hearing Rachmaninov
rolling his fingers through my hair.
I'm summoned, by my,
now, inherited companion
So my lonely piano screams

"Come play me"
T's time to take off my long cloak
To rock and roll my rusty fingers
I'll rattle by the jazz stand
Once I find the blinking key!

Grandmas Ghost Returned

She did it again, jumped out her photograph
This time, she was screaming at me with aghast
She's trying to tell me something
I recently visited her old house by the seaside.
I nearly rang the doorbell

"Twas my seaside haunt, where I picked seashells
from a seashore, as the tides turned.
Underneath the pier was fabulous fun
I'd ride horses along sandy beaches
Gallop in the pouring rain
Soaking wet, I'd put my horse to bed
Then cycle home on my red bike
It's still intact that bike
Found it in my dead mothers' cupboard

So, as the dead scream
I wonder what she's trying to tell me?
Her daughter, my living aunt has got the hump right now with me.
Question me on that workaholic next time around?
Don't forget to dance you dull ones
Your time will run out
I'm not one to mince words

Do what you love
Money comes from lord Jesus jewels

Heartbreak Island

An Island in the sun,
holds a curse on it for lovers.
Young or old.
Makes no change to rules from old timers doing time in witches' misery.

Wear yellow flowers in your hair.
A protection veil that might block the spell weavers.
A touch, but not much.
Time for you to do a runner with your lover.

Don't eat anything hot
Peppers have poison, it's just a clue.
An invisible witch resting on an old broken easel.
She's haunting the bar.
Her eyes are on you.
An old white witch under a safe Jamaican hub
In another nightclub told me so.

It's not an old wife's tale.
It's true

All who ride white ships over there who are in lover's land.
Sadly are under a curse on quicksand.
Like honeymoon dreamers' hand in hand.
You find your marriage is on the rocks,

Your girlfriend is under the chopping block,
before you can put a ring on her finger.

So which island in the sun holds the curse I hereby ring bells on?
I'm not going to sing it out loud
or I might sink again into another evil pirate's banana tree.

Contaminated Contamination

We are all contaminated just by being born.
I blew my trumpet on seeing the ghastly wiry words from press off the lower garter.

Look here don't put more people in bleeding fear of going down the road
Honk, honk, you're a toad.

I checked my garden heads
Last night the bulbs I planted deep down in a front garden ditch.
I blooming well-loved getting my hands covered in dark earth with crawling worms.

Listen up you blonde big belied beer munchkin
A politician on the plane to Ukraine.
I've got an old auntie in that land.
So burst your party balloons.
Don't be tempted now by Russian vodka.
Or polish tonic just across the red line.
I blurt it out loud.
I'm getting my knickers in a twist in the morning mist.
Listening to you fat lot arguing about number ten.

Gordon Bennett's tapping me on my shoulder
I did find my knickers in my Scottish porridge.
I think my black dog rescued them behind my behind.

I don't drink to sink a cats tail myself.
One beer I'd be on the floor singing knees up mother brown.

On putting on my dancing shoes this morning,
After being tempted to buy a paper on the news shelf.
One look at its front page.
I headed out fast back to doggie land in my own home made animal land.
Passed by a limping man.
I said ' would you like to borrow a stick?'
He was stone drunk.
He avoided my eyes.
I could see his trousers were inside out,
I never said another word.
Instead I giggled on route home.
My porridge might get cold and I don't want any more knickers landing in my breakfast fiddles.

Three Men in A Bed

Three men sneaked into my bed apparently.
I was oblivious to this event.
I had no idea what was going on.
I was flat out between the sheets as these male creatures craftily wrapped themselves into various corners of my bed.

I'm in a new bed now.
I abandoned my upper quarters, a boudoir with a French stylised balcony.
upon giving my keys to that room to my young Italian stallion.
One son of mine,
the aftermath of an Italian romance.
I was once bitten whilst in London town by an Italian.
in-fact....
.... I got to go to Rome too at a later date.

I was only told about the three male creatures in my bed whilst I was in dreamland when I took coffee with two of my fine stallions this morning.

Their names are; -
Bingo
Aston
Spartan.

Guess what?
They are my dogs.

The Hotel Porter with a Sly Eye Halloween collection

The brown faced man
Opened his can
It was full of worms
He'd been slung over the reception desk
By none other than my London soy,
with a hairy chest.
He had to let my Sumer lovers cover out the bag
Or he'd have been sacked as I was backstabbed by Count Dracula
on the seventh floor
Even though my lovers room number was 4.

My grinning lover rubbed both his greedy hands
He thought he'd got off my hook!
Oh, no baby. I was around the corner with my dashing
coat.
Just the night before when you bent Madame Banbury
Over your knee
I saw through the entrance of phoenixes long electric opening
doors
I thought to myself as I truly observed
Shall I rush up to 4 on the seventh floor
Bang on my counts door?
I thought it all through
Instead I decided to go hide behind their 4D door

I've had more to scream of than madam Seville
Yet, I'm using the dashing blonde msn
My new elf I've ridden on floor nine
The same hotel
And the brown faced man told me all
He'd no choice my spy is Count Dracula's private eye

Incidentally I'm booking number 4 D to get over my new counts knee
Tonight by four
Mary, Mary, quite the contrary
Booked that room where my count ripped off the tart's knickers
Before outing her over his left arm
So that room is now my London erotic crater for all my screaming orgasms on call by my spinning yarn
Mary she's on my other arm!

The Spitting Dragon

Continue your venomous spitting lark
With long tongues all dried up from hissing on Marylebone floor.
Deep within your dragon ladies' lips you dropped venom
She abandoned her dragons who art made of a brand named
"swine wine ".
as cursing tongues rip into those dragons that spoke a thousand
lies
God bless your weary head and blue eyes that are blind

We're All in The Same Can of Worms

Everything is upside down
The world has gone insane
Even if the men wearing pink pyjama's get grannies slippers on upside down
I doubt they can unplug this one

We got loonies wearing red white and blue
French presidential campaigns gone down the loo
Our men at the top meet face to face under African lace
The worms in charge are laughing their socks off
We're all stinking broke

So just put the bills in the black bin and sin
Say, see ya later Alligator I've got to run to class
Class number?
Let's all go back to school
break some flipping rules
If we're all poor there's no one to sweep the floor
Attishoo!
Where's your handkerchief darling?
London Bridge is falling down
See ya on the other side

The Man with The Pipe

The man with the pipe had no wife.
Once upon a time he pretended to be in wedlock.
Let your tongues drop now.
For high above in the air I see a cow.
A flying cow in no uncertain terms with wings.
Be more honest than that man's pipes smoke rings.

Blow them as he will.
There be more honesty within those smoke sultry rivers cascading into thin air.
Than the lies he breaths from an old well with a tuned tongue.

First class he flies over Caribbean skies.
I sat staring into the midnight sky.
Just t'other night.
He in first class left London at last.
A fine tune sings God Save The Queen.
For she our Queen rests her feet upon ending dares within her diary.
Our Queen and that man.
The one with the pipe.
Had one thing in common.
They didn't meet at Scarborough fair.
No, was another meeting of minds on horses.
Pipes in mind.
Royal enclosures.
Breath while bearing the fruits of thy labour.

For Ireland awaits our Queen in due course.
As do Castles standing still.
In the northern quarter.

Pipe smoke filters by palm trees now.
Our dear Queen has her head on a label at many international flight paths.
Even those on golden sands.
The British empire is more the merry gentleman of pipe smokers' dreams.
Lands cascading gold from slave driven pirates toasting wealth in artificial seams.

I do hope you all recall the night of when the balls roll

Artificial Beggars

What has now came to pass
Is wealthy beggars wearing masks
They're the finest con men in the land
Secretly loaded with big busting wallets
Wearing all designer brands underneath their old bomber jacket
Hanging out at illustrious dens
Always circulating high end
Five star restaurants outdoors will be pinned on their secret map
hidden under a battered Louis Vuitton cap
A few wallets clipped tightly to holes in worn jeans, but
nowadays even design's high end ate into looking rough trends.
Don't be fooled by a bleeding leg
Stage props on sale on Amazon's tail
Hit the theatrical prop list
Anything goes turning themselves from clean shaven men into
dirty looking patients on the run
Don't be fooled by some as some play a double game
They got more bucks wrapped up under that cap
Be it pinned in with rusty safety pins
They in one way or t'other are modern Robin Hoods
Yet, they don't give to the poor
On that fort we need to look through rose petal glasses
The tribe of new beggars is a smeary one

Send Me the Key to My Cell Now

Send me the key to my cell now '
You promiscuous lizard who put me through hell
Send me the jail key first class
Royal Mail isn't as fast as DHL direct.
Want a bet on whose more direct?
Don't go overboard to take the sweat

Please make an effort to drive to a postal dropping joint
On the sunny side of north side of the beach
It's where all the red eyed people high on weed meet at quarter to three.
Before they get robbed by the bar
Or double paid the waiter's tip

Hiding away in your land of sinners arcades
Where rich choose sluts and get laid
' Send me the key to my cell'

I've set myself free
I'm on no rich man's knee
I'd rather get laid by a beggar wearing burnt holy heather

His holiness is more authentic than your wallet laden with dancers who stripped off their knickers
I don't buy old numbers
You hide them in London
I think I recall number 23

Madam B won't do a double eyed dirty on me

Daddies wandering underneath his secretaries' tits
' send me the key to my cell '
NOW

The Hamburger Man (adult humour)

He loves his jerk
Yet, treats women like hamburgers
He has so many varieties of fillings
That the beefy parts get overridden
With all the extra female knickers in between
The layers of really succulent fleshy ones
They're sprinkled with ketchup sauce.

His varieties of tomatoes are usually in top drawers.
Signify the piece of cucumber sucking a vaginas skin
Droplets of organismic fluid weep
For each female piece of prey
Be another laying piece of prey to keep

There be no point in 'The Hamburger Man ',
keeping a little black book!
He wouldn't know where to look.
He's conveniently forgotten
The rosy night you spent on top floor four D
Just like British cups of tea
Where the teabags float

Each piece of flesh
Is just another burger, or another toy to hook.

Don't be alarmed 'Nymphomaniac's
mean no harm!
Eat while you can.

Chicago Boots

I ended up in Chicago's glowing ball
Where windy storms died down
We had a sunshine cloud sprinkling with rainbows
A four-day ball in a hotel, top floor.
With my youngest son in my coats pocket.

I had to wind him up a bit.
We've got to tuck our kids up in safe places,
as travelling with children,
can be mighty expensive.

I hid my boy in my pocket.
A long blowing coat that glittered like gold.
On blowing my necklace whistle
My son would pop up
Like a balloon.
This way, I could smuggle him through security.
Without those long nosed American security guards
Going through my bags.
I'd rather they keep their hands to themselves
Away from my children

I forgot all about my magic stiletto long suede boots
Lo and behold, the tips got stuck.
I thought, I had my little monster in my coat pocket
All tucked away.
But, blow my whistle, or my hidden trombone, as I,

went flying over backwards.
Caught my magic stiletto boots heels 👠
Inside the belt
Those moving floors where you're locked up like criminals

My whistle went off
Out of my magical coat pocket
Popped my son
He raised his top hat, towards the security guards plump astonished face and said.
' A true delight to meet you Sir, my mother Doll and myself, are just flying into do the Chicagoland spin. Have you ever tried the dance?'

Three Cross Dressers

Henry was married to Barbara
Barbara was a secretly a man
But got away dressing female night and day

They'd married
Henry and Barbara after her sex change
She went all out
My aunt was a nurse
A London clinic private beauty queen
Not NHS
She wore seamed stockings
Underneath her nursing dress
One day my aunt said to me
" she'd found his balls in a bucket "
After the chop!

Henry had a secret lover called Clark
Al three dined by Noah's Ark pub
by the strand
At quarter past ten
Usually the Italians in chancery's stepped in
Well the boys backstage knew the numbers
To
everyone's secret pin

Strangulation In the Dark Side

They're trying to strangle you
None of us can sit on swings in playgrounds anymore
They'll catch us in a net before roasting us for supper,
.You're losing your mind you can't move around.

The drug cartel is good for hooks to make you hooked onto a hell road.
Now they look like queens compared to their previous plot using tangerines full of poison.
Hung them top shelf.
You never noticed the for sale human heads mixed up in the fruit shelf, did you?

Crimes weaving basket
You didn't want to pose for the metal rock magazine. half-naked with long Johns.

The presidents have cream crackers early morning spying on you via 5G.
From the Aruba striptease bar.
It's on palm beach.
They got stranded their last night under a pole dancers stare.

The French snails are wagging garlic tails while sniffing cocaine.

The devil is weaning his coat made from sheep hair.
He tipped them off his own milk machine

It was in the bingo hall by the beach bar.
You sat watching balls roll.

Cartels are sniffers with hardcore puts
Tying you up
The temptations you're hallucinating before you get out of jail,
Will you survive without flesh if you get bail?
Try a blow-up doll they sell downtown.
Face it you're monsters in flesh.

An Evening Deck

The devils laid a black jack
Carting a dead dude.

Broken bones hang on to busted legs.
Till you get dragged to dead men row.

Bullet holes still seen by the naked eye of a late-night stripper.
Just off a pole in the road
Many soldiers stand waiting for the bell ringer.

Standing still
what's the next hack on the card decks drill?
Were they too drunk to deal under the table?
Some hit a bottle of vodka liquor going numb
So pain can sustain our fate.

The girl upside down will love a burnt man.
She only hung with her gang instead of running away with Sam.

Death becomes us all
Do it in style or live to the right of your rifle.

Country Bumpkins (Track One)

One day I took a deep plunge down under
I stepped within a countryside bin
I thought, country bumpkins might be more
"up my street."
Rather, than dull eyes staring from
flat computer screens
They're great for hiding one's interiors, thought I.

Tied up in city hubs with shiny white shoe laced dudes.
Where the artificial people hide scars
There wasn't much to amuse.

Perked up white collar people
Walking with polished black leather pointed shoes
Clicking umbrellas through cities paths
onto grey dusty streets.
Or incomplete back alleyways with dustbins over laden
Weep to be emptied to be refilled.

I signed up on a countryside site,
must be nine months gone by I took that track.
Bit my thumb initially
Some stomach bubbles rumbled a wee bit
Opened up a country crate
I discovered quite a different box within

Round two of this storyline
will be on track
soon as I pull off
Smelly boots
I'm in between tracks right now

A Sporting Life

My feet tiptoed in Japanese sandals,
original from an unexpected trip to Japan.
My top bodily parts roped up inside in a kimono, original.

Happened I am having a spring clean.
That time of year to go through all one's gear.
Out with the old in with the new.
I have enough robes to paint myself red white black or blue.
Looking forward to tie up my limbs once more in fine cloths I gathered through travels over time.

Love affairs hanging on lines that were never said.
Instead swept under old carpets, as my lovers can't look me in the eyes.
Honesty runs a needle through rivers where veins of liquid evaporate into clouds only to fall again like the rain does.
How love does simmer to boiling points making our souls jump up and down.

I've reached a bend on the mountain road.
Before me lies a mockingbird singing untold stories yet to unfold.
We are told by the divine eye peeping over our lives.
Run on be wild do not lose the inner child.
Taking up the word of nature's spread like the orange marmalade I spread.
My brown toast is whispering sweet nothings in my ear.
We must cry on burnt toast over all our wreck- less undercurrents.

Load the toaster again.
Second time rounds are usually like stale bread.
The fresh sweep of butter makes margarine cry from the other side of the fridge.

Remember moments we swept ourselves away from grizzly bears trying to prick pins into our wishing well.
Make a wish again, throw it out into the world.
Dance under the light of the moon.
Get on your knees before the Sun God.

Snow falling in April here in London,
while hailstones crying out our earth is dying.

Save us all please Lord, for we are your children.
We will swim, we will climb, we will ride white or black at the front of the back of the hunting pack with hounds.
Yet, let the fox go free.
Have mercy on me, we never set out to murder foxes.

Equestrian games were misinterpreted by the city blind eyed men.
In parliaments den, they know nought yet still drink they're whiskey on the house, at the Hart club.
A Mayfair haunt to pick up hens.
Wiggling tongues get up skirts.
Tighter than hunting dresses.

Letting the fox go free after the ride we rode purely for countryside calling codes.
Chanting with our tribe is but a merry mount.

I count my equestrian trophies with rosettes creased from the box I untwisted.

One might fall if we do not encompass our energies, over the fields far away.
For all sports pass-times are disguised by human pleasures.
We mount again us the merry-men.
Ladies in saddles with skirts where none can see under for, we have our garters hidden under lined cloth.

A magpie sings, I waltzed wearing my kimono with Japanese clogs dancing along in the spring air.
My hair in a turban of course.

Life is a dance.
Do not miss the footsteps or you may miss the chances of new glances.
One look may lead to another romantic brook by the old shed.
Love to be made, plenty of heather up there in Scotland calling in midst of morning mists, as the clouds twist.
Life continues to dance.
Dance on sweet people for the thistles always come out eventually, with a few scars.
Scars well worn by battles we bleed for.
We have a few more on the horizon ahead.
Drink up to the next round.
Have a merry dance. Springtime is upon us.

Second Stanza the Fly

I've got three bottles
Of fly zapping killer spray
I've dressed in pantaloons
Protection of my loins
I'm armed up to top
my brownie caps covered in repellent
With my Sainsbury shelf stingers
Don't think you homing in on my farmers yard
It's stingers time before my bucket skins you by bleached water

Under The Prickly Thistle

Most of the people are terrified of even spiders!
Black or hairy.
As thistles prick or scratch one's skin
In unknown ditched dumbbells.

Ring a phone
Is anyone home?
Most people get planted in ridiculous places
They've outgrown familiar faces

They create a safe
They get stuck in
Never growing from within
Blinded to what is sin or God

So far afield they stare at films on television screens
But they never move off their chairs.

Familiarity be a skilled contortionist.
they get locked up in mud baskets.
They don't see through un-smudged windows.
They hustle along in a dead song
Possessed by dull familiarity

On the lower channel
Find me a person who can stand holding a poor man's hand
whose wearing gold!

Shuffling amongst red herrings
A Honky Tonk Man
Has harder skin
To withstand thistles or the ivy's curse

In Heavens Name Number Ten

In Heavens name, do you think we're your blinking guinea pigs?
for your London Las Vegas spinning wheel?

My eyes nearly popped out on hearing the radio presenter announcement.
Apparently, your conservative party were all partying knees up mother brown _ after telling us to stay locked up indoors last Christmas.

One of your men who got reprimanded for whizzing off to his bit on the side in an English den.

He got caught hands hot on the wheel by the press, before he had to time to unzip his trousers.

Now some sections of Europe are going mad.
Whilst Green Hills of England won't do what you ever say again Mr long John.
Do pull your pants up straight.
Your political lies are transparently dull.

Good Old British Farmers

It comes to pass my father's father on my Ukrainian family belt.
Was a farmer.
Arch-Eye.
A truly Scottish term that many a Scotsman will be calling out on this freckled morning.

Henceforth, be it all but simply under stood,
Apart from artistic genes going nuts about the state of play herein England's fine lands.

One thing I learnt over time buds whereupon I hopped over jumps on my horse.
I'm also an equestrian, just filling you into my bubble.

The country folk, farmers or grooms to the lords and fine ladies sitting having eggs and baked beans on their country estates.
Served over easy by the likes of 'Gordon Bennet'
You know what I mean?
Well, the country folk don't take no nonsense from townies.

Townies, being a country label for you high up pompous snobs who think you know how to rule this land.

I tell you this looking you straight in the eye Boris.
You ain't getting off the hook this time.

No the country folk are certainly not country bumpkins.
Where will you plant your seeds?

In all my years, whereupon I myself fought many tedious battles due to your stinking bent rules.

Bent, you're all sleeping in the same tent, but not on Shropshire counties rules.

Moreish Cream Eggs

The Cadburys chocolate eggs are out and about.
Besides the shop cashier.
Staring you in the eye.
' Eat Me Now '.
They're out on the hunt.

All wrapped up in shiny foil.
The eggs are hunting you down.
They need your blood.
They want your tongue to slide inside yellow yoke.
Cream cheese is off the cards
Cadbury's eggs have come out to play.

Suck the chocolate cast with spells right down the back of your throat.
Suck it slowly.
Let it slide around under your wet tongue.
There's nothing quite like a Cadburys egg.
I'm about to suck one down
upon my wet hanging tongue

Only In My Dressing Gown

Only in my dressing gown
I had nothing else on underneath
It was a fancy apartment in a top London quarter
You threw me out half naked
I didn't even have my purse with me

It was in the early hours
The guests were asleep
The porter on the lower floor raised his eyebrows
But they didn't meet eye to eye
He turned them over to blind himself from my lack of clothing.

He put it all down to lovers quarrels
Then he opened the fancy street door
I needed some air
I was going to have to walk naked half dressed in London city night air
Be it was summer
It's freezing cold if you haven't even got your knickers on

Tried to compress my sorrow
My inner fear
I needed to hang about several hours till daylight doth sprout

Being so posh that neck of town
I walked around half naked
Fortunately my nightgown looked neat

My slippers were dainty pink
I never looked like a sliced up shredded woman externally

Put it down to stage fright
I never caught that bug

The witches in Greenwich

I've moved myself to lower quarters
Nearby feminine rats.
That stick their cursing tongues out.
A neighbours thread weaves
To strangle me under her mask.

These female human rat fangs breathe out lies,
but my black dog drops his poo right in their front garden.

Pulling Strings

Eye for an eye.
I Hereby say ' hi'.
Good morgan. Good morning.
Howdy I guess in U.S.
Bonjour in Paris.
Spanish is not on my table.
Never jumped into the captain's arms.
On that ship stinking of pirates.

The sad end of the stick in my morning unwinds t's this.
' Hissing serpents with slime filled concealed debaucheries of concealed tricks.
Climb around my painted toes
Upon the dirt mud they lie slime bags they are.

Twitching noses.
Criminal minded sliding humanised serpents slither.
Trying to search for an opening gate to my tomb.
Being of the dirt bag types.

The only way they believe they get inside my room in my tomb.
Is to use other men to open me up.

So what sits underneath my cover now?
A bunch of more bleedin swines to knock on wood.
Got the castle front gate locked, but these slimebags at this end of

town.
Need my horse to gallop straight past their sour house.

Black is the best in animal power beds.
In my opinion anyway.
White is fine, but more for my next wedding line.

Lost count now, on marriages I had I mean.
Got to catch up with Elizabeth Taylor.
She got eight.
A number three will do to tie my horse up.
I'm a roaring lioness.
Got to unlock those slimebags down the road.
Knock, knock.
'Any devil in?'

I'm about to ride my horse to Mr large dirtbags place.
The pirate in there has half not upturned whiskers.
A mighty moustache like Inspector Cleuso.
The one from a Peter Sellars show.

I count my chickens after I hatch them.
Not before.
Blast it I got to smile sweetly.
If I gallop on, I reach a different highway man's bowling pitch.

The Shallow People

There are some so shallow
They are almost blind to the ethics of how to respect
Let alone treat another human being
There are some plastic humans
Who will suck you dry for their own needs
Then dump you at the bottom of the street
As they think they're better than you
It's worse still when it's an old lover
He just screwed you as he'd been nursed better
By my god damn self
For six. Looking weeks
Plus he gave me the stinking flu so I was in bed ten days
The geezer I speak off gave me no thanks at all
Then he went off to have a ball with another lying rat
Once he was well, I mean after sucking me till I was sick green.

He threw me to the dogs then
Then after weeks of my dabbing his forehead
I was thrown away like a discarded toy

I'll go back into my cupboard now
But I'm no longer crying over spilt milk
Damn stinking cheek you slimy sick pig you stink

You won't touch my pale flesh
Once more not for a billion bucks
So shove your mean five hundred quid up your lunch

companions ass!

Not with a barge pole are you touching my temple of virginity.

Let a slave drivers stick whip mark my flesh?

Over the homeless tramps outside Sloane Square

I've locked myself up

I only step out underneath the moonlight

With my black dog

My jeweller awaits you to save my death note

The Creepy Dudes Wife

Yet it be a thousand evil men but use their wives as sucking fingerprints
We have but seen, heard many perverted male beasts
Hurled females underneath their blood sucking claws.

Their dirty sunken minds sniff out innocent victim's
The more blinded their victim is
Often by using their own dried out hormonal bitten but not trice shy pen

Hanging up my dirty now rose scented scrubbed sprinkling clean attire
Better with stains or holes in fabric worn torn from beach running on my toes
No cash to save my feet down the street
There's a few dozen men filing females toes
Alright for some who don't have holes in their shoes
Costs a few dime to get to a cobbler
I tie my shoes with holes up in my spare sock's
We always have odds and ends
Make the most if what you got
It's surprising how my shoes fill my walls
Polished or not yet but yet to be

She turned up the creep's wife
In front of my front garden
She's the female flesh the creepy man was using to spy on my den

That stinking creep already has two birds buttered
Over easy.

Get your eyes peeled before you put on the sunblock

Green Fingers

My fingers are green
Planting the executed bulb heads a few months back
They've resurfaced wearing their hats full of petals
My studio, a room I use my third eye,
Is blooming marvellousness.

Six am, the clock struck ' bzzzz. Wake Up!'
I'm in the loft upstairs with Horus my reincarnated cat.
On a matter of eyes
Horus stared into mine, which are green
Putting on BBC radio three
A newsflash strangles my calm equilibrium Into,
the real worlds...
world of skulduggery.

I'd like to moisturise my green fingers now
Hand cream is a necessity to keep smooth skin
Where's my Johnson and Johnson?

Coffee on the rocks with my new taking heads.

The Sky Is Blue

The sky is blue when I think of you
Just as it's a dog called Blue
Whose tapping my wings
I've shut my wings up
I fly only under the moon

The dogs call me through their third eye
Both Blue without my healing charms
T'was I sent to heal one knight?
Attacked by venom from a singing off key bird

The sky is blue when I think of you
Blue taps on my head
From a telepathic dog chain
Chanting out from country grey clouds
City streets hear your sounds

You're a knight on the other side
Fetch the wood
Light a fire
Prepare your barn
Angels come in all kinds of ways
Maybe, just maybe
I'm one.

In Scotlands Raindrops

So we ran amongst wild shores
Screaming every inch of draining city lifestyle out our paws and veins
Dancing as we are under raindrops from a singing riverbed

Seals drift up to say hi
We dance amongst slimy seaweed
Seeing our paws go numb
Off drips my nail lacquer from artificial city saloon floor's
Slimy, wet, sinking our feet inside natural beds

Seashells sparkle as glittering rocks drift by
Under corners of our tired eyes
Intoxication from the divine

Lost A Rule Book

You remind me of a deflated balloon
Your long brown wand has lost its air
You put words into fancy napkins, of only harmful nonsense
You're trying to outsmart the girl wearing purple pants
She has magic pretty pink ants under her glowing blouse, but you're blinded by bending girls.
However, they're all made up like the ones they gave you at Baker Street at five pm

Coffee Gossip (2)

Your hair will fall out or require a strong shampoo, after you hear this story of my stable life.
In fact since I just survived traumatic shocks of a most peculiar kind.
I sit down right now with a pug on my lap dressed up in red.

I'm dressed in a tight clinging black skirt with an added accompaniment of a silk ivory sleeved finely stylised blouse
Long silver silk cords drip from my top collar.
Due to stormy weather I added a purple beaded cardigan.
To top that finely compressed, after morning stable yard duties.

I ran my German shepherd dog named 'Bingo',
Not that I've ever won a game of Bingo in my entire life.
I was playing musical theatrical charades in a three girl band once upon a time along a south-east coast.
Just so happened in between singing orders.
Butlins camp was on a priority order.
Was a short fling on a three girl swing.
I dropped my reigns temporarily upon that twist in time.
I was however always dancing in dressage frivolets.
Not easy doing three twenty degree circular twists.
On horseback I mean.

By gone days as life flutters by us like butterflies silently landing then fluttering off.

A temporary blush of intoxications.
Going with the stride.

As I sit with my little pug.
Recovering from my morning spreadsheet of chores.
The horses all smiling now.
The dogs grin too.
Therefore amongst my bag of little numbers.
Dressing up felt a treat.
Nice to be neat.

I turned a few heads with my current attire.
Upon my walk to fetch a morning paper.
I assume I have a theatrical look.
A touch of Joan Collins with an Elizabeth Taylor blended cocktail. Perhaps? Nice to dream you're a beauty queen or star.
Not sure what that makes me?

I've returned to red lines with purple as my robes to bang all those slimy swines who tried tip me over the hill.
Purple on the cards.
A regal tune hums across the moon.

Over and out
What's this life all about?

Underneath The Elephant

We stood beneath the great beast
His mighty tusks overreached
On trust

He could have
picked us up
thrown us into thin or thick swamps
where bathing hungry crocodiles swum

We feared not
We knew the spirit of the elephant
Wasn't in the room
Because we were dancing in the African bush
Around camp fires by night to drums
As we threw the big bad world of humans outside
One can trust an elephant more than a cop on the hunt for a crime lord

The Haunted House

Behind my grandmothers back garden
There was a long dark lane
It was a slimy shortcut
Going from one rope to the next bell ringer

There was a big ugly tree
With long old branches hanging overboard
towards an old shed.
The shed was falling to bits,
but it had holes that were large,
Just enough to crawl through.
When you're fourteen
You can still bend a bit.

Digging through cracking wood.
The old shed gave you splinters.
Unless you were quick to squeeze through.
A dusty den.
Littered with cobwebs.
One never intended to disturb the spiders.

Big daddy long legs
Sometimes grabbed you by your hair.
Being top of my gang in crime.
My young cousins were suckers for punishment.
Make no bones about it.
They were called to obey

I was the leader of the gang.
So, it wasn't intended to be a boring game.

An old-fashioned house with crawling ghosts
Was far too tempting to ignore
We're on the move
To meet up with its ghosts
I'll fill you in if we make it through the old shed.
Dead or Alive!

Ha, ahhhh!

The Man with Dark Spectacles

I was sitting all alone on a London train.
I'd danced with my feet lifting off the ground into thin air.

I was wearing flat leopard-coloured shoes.
They look expensive, but they were a fifteen-pound Sainsbury store snatch.

The rest of my attire was autumn colours of caramel with dark green loosely hanging woollen slacks.
London tube riding gear is a wardrobe compartment in itself

Of recent months I used tubes like my underlying veins.
I kind of got stuck in a rat trap.

One mean dude who hangs out in town when he lands from unripe mango tree land.
That mean Caribbean stuffy nosed green fingered moulding with scars on his skin from overriding asses before Viagra set in.

Syphilis was just one of that monster's sex bombs.
So his skin is now stained with holes.
He's old enough to have tempered with all life's duets.

One reason why I'm banging that man on the head.
He uses women as mules.

Then he feeds them five stars before tying them up at the secret bar behind his Belgravia bed.

So when the man with dark glasses got on the train.
Somehow, he reminded me of just how fortunate I'd been to untangle myself from that monster's bedroom.

I did a runner half gallon to the tank.
I'm far away from Mr Mango gone off.
Even though my mates in Negril did send me a free ticket to pose nude for Playboy mag.
Don't worry I shall choose artistic nude stills, after I go swimming naked in Negril.

A Hollywood actor is about to run up the promenade in London Greenwich with me and my black dog by my knees.

Send out a drum roll please

Raindrops In the Night

Pitter patter raindrops on my windowpane
The night clouds are crying all over again.
Breathing fast the storm won't outlast before I'm free.
As catastrophic wind makes my green eyes weep.
Making all the animals run play hide and seek.
All straw warming frozen cows with sheep snoring.
Windowpane raindrops patter pitter pit.

A lock plus a code won't turn without a key.
Can't leave my sheep herd alone in the wind.
A gypsy on the prowl will rob me.
Once I'm done at night.
I Will have to set up camp by a tree.
I've a runny nose because I'm freezing cold
A key turns a code plus a lock without a key.

Let The Music Be Your Light

Enclose yourself away from mayhem and corruption
Don't put on the telly
It's all jargon
Bullshit to sell tabloids
None of the big knocking men are honest hens
Turn away from politics daily news
Just play the blues
Or piano concertos number 9
Beethoven bears is pretty neat
While Back In G
A minuet will make you sweat my out evil hormones

Escape away from the herd of human cows
Don't follow the herd you will go bald in sunken buckets of lies

Break free use the music
Play it loud
Then sing your heart out and dance
We're all free
If you were suckers for misled punishment
you can still get out of jail free

Money is a droplet in a fake man's bathtub
You're rich enough
If you got a good wife
Or a husband wearing a wig upside down

If not then you've wasted your time with zero faced Parker nosed men
Only Parker faces dish the dirt in Russian Roulette

Count My Garter

Have I one garter on or four?
Depends on how many stockings one must wear to fight off the wicked west wind.
I shall raise up my bow and arrows.
Target that English creepy town.
Ashford its name, t's where I stuck my thumb.

On one lucky day I had a cottage in the latest news about town.
' murderer not on the prowl '.
The sweet young girl nailed wandering alone.

Young ladies out there, please lend an ear to a wise owl here.
For my mother's words were duly versed.

T's always a bend in the road one cannot see beyond.
Do not walk home over park's alone.
You're due to be sent to my study at a later hour.
Now, I have to drive down to that scruffy little English town.
Green hills for sure but not without dirty ditches.

I must place flowers on the hot spot
Where the devil tied his knot.

I told the police in the local alleyway they shouldn't let burglars off the hook.
T's many a petty crime goes unattended.
Leading to uncovering real threads.

If only more money plus time was spent on police lines for time.
My jewellery stolen aa well as horse's thrown to the ditch's servants.
Did the cop's help me?
No only the local gypsy danced by my garden tree.

Porridge on The Sofa

I was served porridge a la carte
Sitting on a Chelsea flower bed.

A Knight I worship poured out double cream.
A splash of honey layered over plump oats.
My tongue sung I'm in a dream.

Are we dames finally winning our card game
Chelsea flowerbeds opened.
I'm as happy as the white cat in the upstairs flat

Life is sometimes an amazing dream

Congratulations Pure Jewel

Golden jewels sprinkling down
Like confetti over your sweet wife's crown
I crown your heads
As peacocks 🦚 feathers fluttering in windy destinations
Whilst sweet scented heather sings
From my Scottish hills

Earthy bound as winding roads
Leading to many stations with uncertain destinations
Now you both can stand up proud
You made it to the forty-sixth floor
Only four more to go
To reach the next golden door
Congratulations

A Good Samaritans Wand

I waved my wand
Guess what it's all in the mind's eye
Not the third.
That's our password route.
This money Game
It's all a crime
Just sexless sealed camouflaged pain.

Hear, hear me please, pretty please Sir.
Or Madam, for we finally un-hitched the golden locket.
To genetically incorrect mincing cell beds.

The truth of all true really real gold.
Is thus, this.
Even the white birch tree kissed my nose upon my whispering this
secret while I got tangled up in my long green garden hose
We don't have a ban round my neck of the woods on those
ringing one's toes

The richer are poor as burnt toast
So do you give a hoot?
The truth of it all is.
an empty bank is a full tank.
As in no uncertain words I scream
We don't need a penny from the rich
who dream in ugly clouds off their rockers
They are all being sent
into Scrooge's knickers

Blood Moon Chronicles Coming Soon

Ladies and Gentlemen

May I take my hat
See my hat on my picture on the magazine
It's rather unusual
I may have powers
I lift my magic hat to my art director
chief of :-
' Blood Moon Chronicles
' Coming Soon '
On International Women's Day 2022
I openly curtesy to my lady Victoria
Her art work on board for my poems within
Blood Moon are a phenomenal work of art.

Available by love and light on various magical online platforms in two weeks' time

I return to my horse
to mount to ride to black dog
My new co artist Victoria awaits me at the Golden gate

The Farmers Dark Side

Stick em up John Wayne!
British Farmers are preparing for open games
After a long old day battling with British climates
Marginally feeding our sheep
Little Bo Peep, did but weep
In her red polka dot dress
'Twas a little breezy for down under drawers.
Not quite the farmers got a life
Singing in stick em up drawing wars.

American cowboys better saddle up
At this rate we won't be kidding, when we stand saying
' Stick Em Up'.
Stick what up? I wonder.
In green England hills
I guess we're unaccustomed to Yankee style stuff
Mind you, at this blinking rate.
We better get into cowboy gear.

My father loved a good western
Dad knew how to use a gun
He'd been frontline

Anyone for shooting games?
I'm a vegetarian
I was on strike at Christmas

Lines By the Thames

A few dead men wandered past me under the mist hanging.
Whispering morning chants breathed out their frozen living corpses.
Where are we all?
Are we all dead whilst alive?

Wrapped up to such extent with bodily wraps hiding faces from the hidden virus, that stuck it's claws into this city.

Seems the walking dead is concealed as the living.
Two world's blend both with unknown destinations.

Old sailor's ghost's float amidst the sunken ships.

Hanging chains attached to sidewalks adrift.
Lye isolated awaiting another adventure.

A river full of mystery.
Turns time in history.

My frozen fingertips depict I'm still living.
For surely, we won't think we're dead when we cut the cord.

Maybe we're all dead already?

Unions Up in Arms

Undo your purse strings Sir Transport Minister.
They're not going back to business without a reasonable check-in.
Drivers are tired of all your crap.
Commuters are eating chips without being fried until next week.
We then hit a snarling heatwave.
Train Tracks are laughing now.

Right now two MPs are squabbling over who wins the best seat.
As you pull each other's hair out to pull economic tangles out
with blunt hair combs
Everyone stands, suitcases in hand.
The crime lords are on the run.

Rick knows the money game.
The luscious blonde Liz is a bet and a half.
Gamblers end up broke.
Don't feint with shock
Cheltenham lights are on parliaments right.
Push to the left? Or pull to the right?

Grass Up!

Bottoms up t'was an old fashioned English slogan
One may say chin chin on hosting the toasts
Number ten I'm going to have a good moan about you again
I'm afraid we've got one thing in commons
You PM's and I
Though it be a slanted resemblance
Hellish holes wear pink party knickers
You thought no one saw your pants
Going to the British bog
Is like thus ' boys to the right ', ' girls to the left '.
Ladies don't stand up to pee
We don't see each other's coloured pants
Boys in blue I'm telling you
Competing at the top
Now, see the penny drop
If you're going to drink like fish
In the middle of mask up laws, that you laid down
Then for heaven's sake get drunk alone behind your own closed doors
As I confessed I myself have a string to pull with you dopy liars
Of course your pants were on fire
The press missed the point
Why? They were trying to catch you pulling another porky pie
I don't think we need clowns leading our land
Are you certain you aren't living at Eton half term?
I've got so many holes to pick now on you clowns leading
I won't need to sign up for the circus

Porcupines And Needles

You damn fools
Suited men sitting around Big Ben
How could you put a hedgehog in charge?
I have no words for where back benchers do in time out?
You'll probably find them by the red telephone box parade.
Telephoning weirdos on bookers cards.

They have their wigs made in a back street bar which nearly went
flying last night under the striptease artists eyes.
Their Mrs at home is blind as a bat to what's going on
These men wearing grey flannel suits are two faced
Except on the golf course mate
Out pours venom then
Hey ho aim fire

Dirty conversations with sexually explicit use of verbs
No, they tend not to use healthy herbs
A quick pint or five-star dinner at The Hart Club
Mayfair downtown hides all their knickers now.

Sone of them love to cross dress
All their fancy panties are packed away in a black brief case.
There's nothing wrong with cross dressing
It's just hard to recall what pants they got on for the next Johnson
ball.

Laws in this land?
They tend to be filtered but hung.
The axe comes down

Surely you didn't think a bunch of potato face men could lead this green hill land beholden with secret joints scattered around.

Clamp out your cigarette stubs
Big Ben.
You all have a fag behind the bus stop
We caught you out now.
You stopped on route to your weekly Friday night but on the side.

Gentleman on back benches
There might be a few of you I could stick gluey labels on saying 'over easy'.
That's a good boy
However I'm so aghast with how you create order
The speaker of the house I feel needs a strong whiskey
Be it thank lord God he's no mouse
There all mice on the hunt.
Run Boris run.

That Is the Question

What kind of mood do we want to swing to?
To portray our present paraphernalia going on?
A quick step mixed up with rub a dub dub three men in a tub.
I'm not sure our feet could move to the new rhythm,
It's all so bizarre.
The big heads at top of the ladder all gone stark raving mad.
They all need to see a shrink double time.
I think not even a shrink could cope with our political jerks right now

No offence to my dear Prime Minister but what in heavens name are you on?
Parting the night before our fine Duke Prince Philip's funeral.
My dear Queen had to go to her chapel today with her head in her arms, how she kept her head on is beyond me.

To top the party games the night before mark my word no ordinary burial.
A royal one.
The blue bunch of leaders over here were drinking dancing rubbing their noses on each other's bums.

They forgot all about my dear Queen's Kings funeral.
On the next morning that broke.
We're all broke being conned.
The masked parade is our new show.

I'd give Boris a slap on the face.
If I were in my Queens shoes.
Right hand not left like in the old black and white movies.
I tried it once on a right playboy wimpish man I was but blinded by his sorcery to love.

Then she's got pain to top her grief with prince Andrews philandering.
A prince running around with his uncontrollable balls.
Super Nova plus a touch of coke dipped in gin.
He did so grin while sweating his aphrodisiac smells through his open unbuttoned shirt
Dance through their nose in the Tramp club.
Mayfair, round about town.

Our new dance must be crazy as these super nova twirling aristocrats.
English gentleman, excuse me non- comprehend
Say it in French.
As leaders of this land are stinking grease bags.
No wonder the French are opening their borders.
All hail, let's all go dance down the Champs Elysée fast.
Even French snails are saner.

As far as time for tennis goes.
There's scandal from Australia.
Melbourne to make it blunts.
I got fired at by guns when I once got to a set on film
In Melbourne Australia
No one murdered me

Got straight off a plane
Straight to location
Bang bang
All arms were safe
Bang bang bang
Dance but wear braces like the English gentleman.
They're too Keep their trousers on.

After dark they are used like darts to play ping pong.
You can't think the English wear white handkerchiefs for no interior motive.
Frightfully not good people.
The white hand shake is another message in a pot.

Dance fast before we laugh so much our stomachs burst
We must be sober to drink French wine on the next boat we're avoiding the rattle of immigrants we're going to France.

Dracula Lost His Fangs

There's a man without fangs.
He's done the chop on most of his dangling items.
He used to expose his tools to cut slices of emotional war weaponry.
Solemnly stands like a Prince with a brand title.
On an edge.

Wearing Chanel as a cover.
Invites you all around to lunch at three.
Taps his fingers on a burnt tabletop.
A disguised face, with wrinkles breathing clues.
Getting wet in London rain isn't his time bomb.

Plotting high on a leading edge.
Planning where to hide the bag of poison, currently under his bed.

Tools to amuse.
Life's boring without torture.
He decides upon how to lure his victim, to his quarter.

The clock strikes three.
It's time the bird's feathers are plucked over his knee.
He can't catch the bird without a shotgun armed.
British sports in country games leave guns loaded until next time.

This villain hangs out in dark alleyways
A back street parade lined with strip joints.

I stripped all my fear off after seeing a dancing bell ring.
It's your turn now, not mine.
Turn around, look at him.

Young bird's flesh feels soft to weary aging hands on the brink.
Let's tip out old ink pens in the black bin.

Look through the eyes of the count.
Chopped-off Fangs might be in your Hong Kong noodle soup.
Don't waste the wine, it's blood poison time.
On the table.

Which fork?
It's a five-course meal.
Fried ostrich with eggs over easy.
Don't get queasy.
Counts only spy on you eating.
Blood is the name of the game.
Is he your enemy or your friend?
Mix it all together.
Cocktails have to blend backward before the next bell rings.

The Grinding Road

Every day is a grinding lane
A road we take blinded by yellow ribbon men.
As yokes of eggs crack
opening wide running eggshells combine
as men of crime
Try catch us off guard
Be it one mile or an arm's length.
A glass eyed owl fits in a den
like a pocket full of
Laptops eyelashes bitten by viruses.

The blinding of life's surreal edge.
Disguised paths of men sitting on the edge.
Smeary windows that need cleaning.
Staring through rose tinted glasses.

However much you clean your room
Nothing unsurprisingly can be forever
As birds of feathers dust past
From flying nomadic bird tribes.
Escapism is only one route
Take the bold one
or die in reincarnations
Rhythmic sound.

God Save Queen E

The dragon in between snarls
They do pick their moment duly to unleash the wild dogs.

Big Ben strikes on time
Our dear Queen Lisbeth looks complexed.
She was dressed in dark green
Forgiveness for her son the apple of our eye is often wonky
Only a knight who puts up a fight can be pardoned

Forgive me if I'm being blunt but all the millions thrown
Won't take away a bone from a hungry dog.
I'm perplexed as I wipe my tired moon weeping eyes for
Mothers must be dragons too at times.
I lend you a crimson handkerchief my lady
Yet, I see through your souvenirs
On what King Philip might have advised
T'was such a sticky pudding that one.

The yanks don't take no as an answer
After all they're blooming cool cowboys
At end of a day's woes crossing one's mind
We mothers repent lending our hand to have and to hold
Yet, there be no getting our son's out of jail on bail using pound notes.
The matter at hand is shut but with a lost key.

An old owl says you see
guilt can be hidden with gold
Now the story is never really over
justice must grin and bear its horns first.

Light a fire cracker then blow it out
Parliament's seats to be taken for the next round.
' Are we all ready for the morning papers?'

Gordon Bennet it's too early for a drop of nerve tonic.

Blue Murder

She was a beautiful dancer in London Town
Her belly could wiggle half way around your house
Then back to where you rolled your last joint.
She wore ruby tummy chains.
Hiding her exploding veins.

This tragedy occurred in the nineties,
there's a few gap years in between.
Lying around in between my old can of spreadable margarine.
I sit buttering my bread.
Hearing ghosts mumbling over my head

Around town gossip spreads
souvenirs down memories threads.
I shed my tears upon my handkerchiefs lining.

From doses of crack cocaine,
whizzing around her veins
Her beauty attracted mean male mouses,
making dancing clubs
For overhanging spouses.

Her hangouts were in the best nests in town
But. where is she now?

Murdered in Maid-a Vale
Number sixty-four
Streets a top secret.

Or I'll get shot
on the top floor.

Her body screams through my dreams
She's trying to bust out her death jail,
but lost her keys

There's another ghost beating within
Fiery red breath beating an old tambourine

The other woman,
a jealous number.
never saved her from that strangulation.
The night the boss
of her favourite club
Committed blue murder.

Coffee Gossip

The two blonde women were both clutching onto my skirt.
They hung out together at one of my more fascinating parlours
I'd snatched mighty fast.
A London agent who knew his game.
Got lucky on hitching me.
Cost a fine penny.
Rent deposits in London town still unite fireworks up under my dressing gown.
Just zipped it off after a struggle to get to the sour faced geezer at my morning shop.
A smile from those bleeding clowns who sit at check-out tills wouldn't go amiss.
Afterall, I'd just ridden my white horse through misty winds with flying viruses all in smithereens.

Masked up like Robin Hood on a highway drill.
None applauded as I dismounted.
Extremely gracefully too.
Remember the wind was flying up my skirt.
Oh no, I was not wearing jodhpurs.
T'was a side saddle stride of this day in May.

What a month, for now we have cowboys' verses Indians out on that large playing field.
You must have heard ' John Wayne's ' arrived to assist.
Please don't get your knickers in a twist.
I've got everything under control.

The sailor over the pink boat named Molly knows all his lawyers' secrets.
He told me so t'other day.
Invited me on board Miss Polly.
I smiled sweetly, turned around.
Returned with a steak sandwich spread as my gift.
It be a mighty gift as I was invited upon an original sailing boat.

Don't stress about my horses.
I've stable girls who arrived on duty late today.
Therefore, I had to tick them off with my whip.
Smacked the stables floor with red tempered fury.
Fortunately they obeyed my stance.
Stepping near my neck of the woods requires time keeping to be in perfect pitch.
Unless you want your head in a ditch.
Don't give me excuses.

The two ancient blondes' mouths hung open.
Watched me deliver the steak sandwich on the plate to ' Miss Polly's ' captain.
All aboard I said.
We are waiting at the boarding gate now
Stick your western gear back on fast.
John Wayne's back in town
We do love Indian curry but can't have Indian viruses sticking their necks out around this neck of the woods.

Thou Wicked Lawyer

I am alone yesterday abandoned in a deck.
A space like chair tilted me backwards.
As a sweet goblin appeared like fairy dust to mend my bleeding teeth.
I raise my auburn silky hair.
My face is like white lace but my blood was stained upon my hands as I danced on London City sands.
In the morn at crack of dawn.
Before I was bleeding...

I am in so full up with invisible scars from mountains of blood pressure shed after those evil goblins shovelled me into graves Within their minds.
Yet they went to throw the darts.

Darts now hail cash in another land of rich geezers under blankets.
My evil devil the one who pokes me in the night.
Maybe I'm the master goblins wife,

I fantasised on going under the needle.
No morphine spills in this dance.
The goblin men want my teeth now.
Yet, the King who pays my bill pinned me to strawberry Hill yesterday.

No joke. He played blind man's buff.
The cops were behind a looking glass
Law is not one to mess with.
Be it a bag of caterpillars.

King Harry may be dancing in L A with Princess M.
I'm still doing hop scotch tackling rich bastards after my bottom around Big Ben.

The clock strikes one pm.
The Devil rises late.
He's so many women's bottoms to grab.
I'm the last on the ladder to run away.

I'm no rich man's bird.
Or Devils trumpet.

Phone the goblin.
The court rules you do.
Or I will see your name in lights
Wait and see just what I do.

In The Midnight Hour

Black dog and I will walk
Tonight in the midnight hour!
We're more likely to bump into ghoulish men
We've given up on living dead
We're going to run when the tide turns
After ten pm.

Some dead sailors wake up
Around about then
We might take a glass of ale
If it's still alive and kicking
Rotten forgotten stinking rum
Underneath the underground
Sailors drunken or not
Let's get moving around my plot.

No need for Saturday night dancing in fleshy parades.
Out in Soho or Mayfair floors downtown.
I'll have wringing wet sandy feet instead
In my town.
With dust in my hair.
Thrilled to pieces with ducking worms
Clinging to my boats edge.

A few dunking dives
screaming unpredictable tides

No ghostly dancing
Left me dead yet.

Hoist up on you go your muddy sails
Cracked masts creaking while pulling
A few fallen dead snails
Added extra slime to my hair
What's left over from human thongs.

Ghosts from the past party time
Is only in the midnight hour
Some hours last forever
Let's dance
You don't need no money
Nor your clothes.

Daft News

This might be a touch punk
While blowing breath into my teacup of yet another blend
I encountered in one of my retired handbags
Handbags be an elementary canal to a woman's back door
One never knows quite what one will find
If, for one reason or t'other one changes bag colour.

Did you know?
Tis an old-fashioned etiquette rule
One's bag must match one's shoes
Dressing be an exterior canvas of one's interior layers.
Check it out!

Talk to a woman or a man
Wearing bells on their toes
Without rings on their fingers or right up their nose
One might find one will get a good verb out
A punk rock band might not be silent off stage
If the rings connect.

I was inclined to reveal my Achilles heel
It's not dried up yet

The Overcoat

An English Gentleman's underlining be most hypnotising.
Hereby I say this
My green eyes laden with running mascara after doing a five-minute face paint job to go hopping.

On wearing my green flower shoes
Picked them up cheap at a northern town stall.
Fifteen quid I seem to recall
Everyone's pretty broke in downtown LA
London beggars meet by Big Ben to split the beans.
I was there last night
I was on a frog's private jet.
Green things have wings too.
Hereby the verse drifts.

Having returned to number 10.
No, not with any British MP.
I turned a pile of those down from a sleazy nightclub joint donkey years ago.
Don't ask where it was
I need to keep your knees shaking

He ain't getting in my knickers .,
thank you very much.
My mother hen now residing near Big Ben
She wouldn't allow me to get taken for rides with men.
My X thinks he's painted me red in lying letters to frogs in court

when I fought back to the flower pot men from my sweet number 10.

He was drinking porn hot cakes before he pushed my name into artificial bent backwards child snatchers.
judges' eyes have spiders crawling inside
only concerned with stealing kids to produce
sickened men's talcum powder
Watch out it sold out at the pound shop.

I hopped, skipped jumped back from where the Indian turban man blowed me kisses whistled
I had ten quid
saintly slags for unless we were forced to open our legs by toads
We got our chastity belt on you stinking so called knighted men
I wonder what you did you bent motions to get up to the garter?
Porky pies
I scratch off my running mascara

Picking up where I left off screaming in black pen ink

The English Gentleman still exists
Just ensure he's not an apple crumble assorted mix of Lebanese bricks.
I got sucked in by one of those half-baked tarts a generation ago.

Now I'm in my third lifetime
I have a rather peculiar diary
Indeed so jolly good show I'd but an English old slogan
Add old chap and you incredible Yankees from yank

The American dream
Can adopt a new 'How Ya All Doing?' Think tank.
Not Germans.
I'm not pulling out my teeth for my dentist is sweet

I'm rolling in lists to do to do
I will be back in a hat trick
The silver haired London Queen next door
The photo I push out of my mouth with this little number
He's got his green coat from an X spy

Now that will bring you back for my next bite

Space Flash Station

Hear, hear, come lend an ear to my left ear
overheating a heartbeat from a whispering radio on my shelf.

I couldn't sleep for the life of me.
I am alive most unfortunately for my black list of humans.

Indeed, we all have a black list.
Be it known loud and clear I am not referring to the colour of your skin.
A white skin might well have more red blood.
But a dark skin might well be well blended for roots of our cavemen were of multi- coloured types.

In any case I'm not going down philosophical routes while my clock is back to front.
Therefore I stole a slice of cheese from a larder down below, under the stairs.
A large silver monster it was so still
Opening its mouth I grabbed a slice.
Then I shot back up to upper deck juggling three sleeping dogs who are flat out in dreamland.
No one lets the dogs out around this neck of the woods except me.

So, upon my resting back into my sack to get a few winks.
Radio blurted out a dodgy space news spread.

Read all about it I'm sure in tomorrow's daily press.

'Suddenly In Outer Space', somewhere heading towards earthly spaces. 'Is a very large unknown object '.

I'm wondering if our new space examination over to the far side. A recent new avant-garde mission, by our recent American carousel.
Has raised the dead?

Febzer The Wild Dog

I'm Febzer, chief of my pack. I hereby sit
upon this waterbed to eat
I hold no grudges,
for they've all got to run with long feet

T'was a dirt bag catch,
until I could suck delicious flesh.
Hiding away from my batch of cannibalism

Blood from my prey
drips out my nostrils
It's my heyday!
Bit like ketchup, those peculiar creatures, humans suck on their
pathetic tongues.
I see their trucks occasionally...

On our families' meaty meetings
We need no profiteroles,
as final decisions are made on the run.

Like your final results lye basking
with artificially pumped chocolate cream.
Menus stink up shanty town street
Let's get down to business.

Blind Men Who See

You're blind as bats
Without their nose, but suck poison
All of you monstrous blind oaths
Those who have servants slice their own bread
Give the maid a tip
Whilst thinking about your mistress in the bathroom
You had to hide her somewhere
Or else, the maid will tell porky pies
The tip will keep her mouth shut
As you look forward to opening yours
You might have a loose little penis now
But girls wearing your bills
Do a good blow job
This will suffice, as the woman you love has brains
Plus great legs.
But your legs were a puller in 1949
Probably why you hitched a tired Oxford rose.
Back to blind man's buff.
There's plenty of money in strip poker!

Blind men are not really blind
Those men who can see
They can't see anything under one's skin
It's all a superficial act.
That's why they keep their eyes closed when they speak.
How many orgasms have you had?
When a man can look at you straight in the eyes?

Then you'll know if he's real.

It's simple for men to screw you, whilst dreaming internally of Sue!

Digest this lady with your weekend coffees

Come Inside My Dolls Cupboard

As it's a holy moment in Christ's quarterfinal
We have three more days to be exhausted by shopping trips.

Don't trip over the Christmas doggie bowl
He's got his paws ready to let rip into Santa stockings
Before you forget to leave Santa a glass of sherry underneath your chimney.

If you're living in a glass house, I'm sure Santa will get into your shoes somehow or t'other.
I'm staring into my crystal ball
Reading all about your future just now.

Listen my sweet people of every nation
Whether you're white, brown or a blue alien just passing by,
Behold an international hymn doth ring
As sounds of bells sing out from everyone's smelly laundry basket.
Don't tell me you got a bust machine too.
Stuff Hotpoint. I'm not running you down
But, I'm about to get my second divorce so I'm as broke
as the cat down the road.
I'm still however wearing my fake furs.
Additionally added a slick of red lipstick
I'm not complaining or competing with the cat.
I'm taping my long fingers on a brown table outside

Stuck in a rut.
Don't freak out just add more lacquer to your mop
You managed to grit your teeth on wondering, what the flipping heck is all the fuss about Christmas
After all we need is a church down in town.
Don't tell the old priest any lies.

Sinners win on a first round,
but they don't make the semi-finals.

It all comes out in the wash
Whether you get lumbered with a busy spinning wheel
Or a brand spanking new Bosch.

My style of dressing doesn't do modern laundry justice
For I'm still dressing like Mary Queen of Scots!
Not on her day she had her head off.

Tit for tat, take this pie in your face
You good for nothing weasel!
His names rather tame
Squeaky likes to wind up old broken clocks

The Red lipstick

A tube of trashy red lipstick appeared yesterday on my table.
A product Ms ugly cow, an unattractive clinging female left behind.
One of those worried about being left on the shelf.
Dig their claws in..
Don't give a dam whether he's taken.
Thick as bricks.
These kinds of tarts aim fire.
Clutch your mam by his attire quickly.

The lipstick mark on his collar.
Accidently on purpose.
Just turned up one day in two nineteen.
That year that cow was meowing around my quarters.

Lipstick on my table last night.
Her brand not mine.
I don't use cheap rubbish.

Two timing time.
Name of the wine.
Is my intelligence threatening?
A dumbbell is much easier to orgasm.
No challenge though?
Just another piece of flesh to amuse.
Hope she remembered the planes flying.
Means we're all.in the same bucket of wine.

Older dragons are more adept at fooling.

An afternoon scream before you dig another stream.

Don't forget your lighter.

Hampstead Heath

Full of stranger's I didn't know.
I was invited by a beautiful black Goddess.
Those kinds of numbers that have cracked life's secret bar codes.
Her silken woven quarters were a vogue designers' drug.
Sitting on a velvet sofa a male number slid in closely to my physique.
Shared a drink.
My head went dizzy.
Standing up I regathered my senses.
I filed before I landed in a stranger's bed.

The streets of Hampstead in the deep night air.
I'd left my purse behind in my desperation to run away.
Stopped a stranger to borrow their phone.
Ended up having coffee a long way from home.

Running sometimes leads stray dogs to other kennels.

Yvette

They'd never believe it those hackers,
that I'd use my own name as my username.
I like to play tricks with fraudsters.

Lifting my top hat, there's a bunny rabbit popped out.
My chocolate easter egg is all in my tummy honey.

Just one, break a leg.
I needed a spare in case a stone needed for my grave.
My left legs dead,

Screenwriters pins and needles.

Broken Glass

On the second day of indulging in artist den hysterical cleaning.
You need a stiff drink to join me in exploring this den of mine.
Even I need a drop of gin and tonic to reduce my nerves to a calm state of mind.
Never realised I'd been quite so outlandishly naughty.
My lingerie bags are bursting.
Screaming 'let us out'.
That geezer I loved sure had a real deal in blackjack games with rocking birds.

I never knew in New York City, birds was a line for hitching girls, until one day one New Yorker tried to work his way into my knickers.
Fortunately it was online.
Posed himself as some big timer.
As they all do to grab your garter locket.
Once you're inside these big timers pockets.
They add you to the crowd.
Each hitching pitch moves their chosen numbers.
Where you're pitched is up to them.
You're a piece of flesh, nothing else.

Think twice before falling for lines of falsehoods.
If they're being true.
T's just to get their honey.
Dangling money part of the game.

Afterwards once you're no longer amusing.
You're on a charter flight to Timbuktu.

You've clocked on.
Clued up.
Gulp, gulp.
Swallow some water.
Were you temporarily blind?
They say love is blind.

A piece of glass cracked loudly in my downstairs bathroom.
I'd just staged the house.
Supposedly evil spirits are escaping.
Maybe I'd left the downstairs loo more susceptible to devils I'd trampled down.

So happens I was manoeuvring light weight furniture around.
Crash the glass broke from a sketched print by an old artist friend.
He used to drive me around the bend.
Now he's still sitting in water.
I'd sold his art for more than a quarter.

The old money currency sings hymns.
Only a short while ago.
We used to have half-pennies, with quarters.
Slowly all burnt as cards with high charges.
Banker's forgeries.
Do you think we are blind to skulduggery?
Measly measures from scrooge's fingers.

I'm leaving the broken glass now on the floor.
Closing that door.
Time for a cup of tea.
The black dog isn't too happy either.
That spirit is trapped, trampled on by all my knocking knickers hopping.

Has the rabbit in the hat got stuck?

Abracadabra.

A Human Experiment

In the year two thousand and nineteen.
In numbers, speaking 2019.
A few huge giants sat around a round table.
Rubbing their hands together, as money was their only prerogative
Neither planetary well-being or the human beings residing within, being of any concern to these giants.
For hunger for power was all that lay inside their mouths.
Long tongues they had indeed, which hung out panting like a wolf does after the animal has eaten.

These kinds of giants hide behind gold castle doors.
So, on one day at one of these monsters round table meetings.
A plan was connivingly contrived to reduce the human race in numbers by creating a virus from an animal.

The giants grinning with their tongues hanging longer than the Suez Canal, had other ideas alongside their cunning evilness.

Upon much meaty discussions showered with black pepper sauce over succulent pieces of meaty flesh.
The animals they'd shot right on their own doorstep, of the chateaux.
Usually lining hills in high northern planes on planet map quarters.
Terrains used amuse many hunters.

Fat bellied men, who eat to amuse the giants.
Servants cart each animal corpse to hide until the tide turns, which arrives at every beat in time to skin peel corpses.

Immersed in beasts dancing creating eviller using our planets waves of wonder.
The giants scratched their heads.
Thinking as earlier said, to reduce numbers of humans would be good use for their stomachs aching for human flesh to rip to shreds.

Now the giants had another plan.
A virus from animals would be a key to power.
Filling their stomachs on the way.
Dead humans would never be buried.
Families would never be able to pay funeral costs.
Shipped off instead to their secret gold dens where more experiments could unveil.
On the humans' brain

A requirement of brains was absolutely an imperative requirement.
Insertions of the kind required to dissect minds of humans to absorb clues they required with scientists they'd paid a good whack who they'd hired.

Evil giants gave buckets of gold to lock scientists up they needed to have and to hold.
To do as they were told.

Using media as pockets to send out lies in forgeries.

Dissecting what they required from minds of dead corpses.
The needle was thread.
The eye of the needle took a little time to find.

Goals being one of exterminating the dark race.
Being one they wish to reduce to emplace.
They're all racist because they are scared cats.
Dark races hold much talent.
Giants don't listen to good music only sleazily dull stuff like pornography with front page pussy cat spreadsheets.

Upon the human dissections, genes are required from bodies of young females to create artificially inseminated humans using embryos and sperm.

As the snakes move, lock up your daughters.
A whole pile just got the axe under forty.
They've plenty of young men already.

Cheers to the giant, we got you all mapped out mate.

April 2021

Printed in Great Britain
by Amazon